MEMORIES OF A
DIFFERENT WORLD

Charles Gallagher

About the Author

Flying Officer G C K Gallagher DFC 191699.
Born at Wilford Rectory, Nottingham in 1924.
In 1930 his father moved to Dartmoor to become vicar of St. Petroc's Church at South Brent, Devon.
Educated at Montpelier School, Paignton and Blundells School at Tiverton in Devon where he became Captain of cricket.
Joined the RAF from Cambridge University through the University Air Squadron in April 1942.
Charles has been married to Mary for 62 years, has 3 daughters, 7 grand-children and 2 great-grandchildren.

First published in Great Britain in 2015 by
Charles Gallagher
www.memoriesofadifferentworld.uk

A CIP catalogue record for this book is available from the
British Library.

ISBN: 978-1-9995841-0-8
also available as an ebook

2

This book is typeset using Atomik ePublisher
Printed in Great Britain by Belforts Printing Limited

A note from the Author

It started off as a bit of a hobby a couple of years ago - jotting down a few memories, thinking the next generations might be interested - and evolved, with much encouragement from the family, into a book. Memories of people and events I hadn't thought of in any detail for 70 years.

It has been a wonderful experience.

In memory of those I had the honour to serve with and for those who gave their lives, my small contribution in keeping their story alive. I hope you will enjoy reading it as much as I have enjoyed writing it.

Charles Gallagher

Acknowledgements

Kate, my daughter – for her dedicated work in transcribing and shaping of the book and the many hours working together on the text. Also for her help in the computer world of which I know nothing. My debt for her help and guidance throughout the book is massive. Without it 'Memories of a Different World' would not exist.

Rosanne, my daughter – for her help in turning early memoirs into the beginning of a little book.

Mary, my wife and Caroline, my daughter – for their help and support various whenever asked.

David, grandson – for the website – pure magic – serious excellence in a world in which I am totally illiterate.

Rosie, granddaughter – for her first class photographic contributions.

James Macfarlane – who has given so much and so generously in time, thought and help in the process of publishing the book.

Emma Graves – for the superb final production of the book.

Abigail Lovegrove and William Howard - for working on the various stages of production.

Contributions

Wing Commander Stuart Hatzel and FT/LT Martin Wintermeyer, both of RAF 76 (R) Squadron – for their exceptionally interesting and kind Forewords.

FT/LT Mac MacFarlane DFC (Skipper) – for his account of two training flights and five operational flights – an encyclopaedic memory amongst many other great qualities.

David Hewings – for his article on the Battlefield tour and much of the arrangements for a wonderful day.

Elodie Lecrosnier – for her thoughts on the Normandy landings and beautiful painting of the battle area.

Foreword

Given command of all RAF Weapon Systems Officers under training at RAF Linton on Ouse in February 2006, I knew our students would quickly find themselves flying Tornado GR4 aircraft on perilous operations over Afghanistan just as Charles, Mac and their crew members had flown Halifax aircraft over Germany some 70 years previously. The qualities of RAF aircrew have varied little over the years. Aircrew need to work hard, bond as an effective team in hardship and maintain a sense of humour which can, admittedly, appear a little macabre to non-aircrew. The qualities of the young men and women who fly on RAF operations now are instantly recognizable to their forebears. To help them realize this, it seemed entirely sensible to submit a formal request to the Air Force Board for our Tucano squadron based just outside York and known simply as the Tucano Air Navigation Sqn or TANS to re-badge as 76(R) Sqn. This was granted on 7th May 2007.

The benefits gained from drawing on 76 Sqn's wartime heritage and the introduction of a warfighter ethos during training was immense and immediate. By far the greatest effect came from our students meeting with veterans under the auspices of the Squadron Association. Gentlemen such as Charles, Mac, George and Bert regaled today's aircrew under training with similar wartime stories to those recorded in Charles' book. In doing so, the veterans transformed for a few minutes back into those young warfighters about to climb into a Halifax bomber ready to take off from Holme on Spalding Moor for one more operation. Naturally, they gained instant and enduring respect and understanding. Our students were not the only ones to succumb to the 'veteran effect'; their instructors who had fought over Afghanistan, Iraq, and the Falklands, and who had sat watch in forward West German bases during the Cold War, also gained immeasurably from our new friendship with old 76 Sqn comrades.

I commend Memories of a Different World to all readers such that they might enter the world of Charles Gallagher sailing to his South African aircrew training base at the ripe old age of 19. It is a world where Service comes before Self and only Resolute courage sees you through. Those same qualities are still much in need in today's world and, luckily, in the modern RAF much in evidence.

By Wing Commander Stuart Hatzel
Officer Commanding 76(R) Squadron

As a current serving member of the RAF I have been an instructor on 76 Squadron at Linton on Ouse. It is also an absolute pleasure to be involved with the 76 Squadron Association, which includes sadly dwindling numbers of squadron members from earlier generations.

The 76 Squadron motto since 1919 has been 'Resolute' throughout the squadron's years and up to the present date. The men and women who have served the squadron for almost 100 years have in my view indeed been determined, purposeful and unswerving in their loyalty to their country,their squadron and to each other.

I have never been so proud to be associated with such a 'band of brothers' and feel honoured to call many of them friends. Unless you have experienced life on an active squadron it is difficult to appreciate that the squadron is your family during both good and challenging times.

I met Charles Gallagher at RAF Odiham in 2012 at a special occasion when he and his WWII Skipper pilot, Walter (Mac) Macfarlane, were reunited with a front-line RAF aircraft MP-Q, their trusted aircraft call-sign from their 76 Squadron war years.

We were privileged on 76(R) Squadron to have our RAF advanced Tucano Training aircraft painted in the livery of 76 Squadron from the war years. Mac and Charles' was the last aircraft to be painted in its WWII service colours and it was a very special moment to see them both reunited with Q-Queenie ('her') after a gap of nearly 70 years!

Although the aircraft from the two eras are very different, Halifax VI to Tucano, their purpose remains the same for the men and now women who flew them.

Having personally served in the RAF over the past 30 years, it is clear that the fabulous example set by Charles, Mac and their crew 70 years ago in Q-Queenie, is still being carried on into the RAF traditions of today. The aircraft may be faster and more technically advanced but the individual courage, commitment and personal abilities required of their aircrews remain unchanged across the intervening generations.

This is an outstanding book both as a magnificent historical record of some of Charles' escapades but also a fine source of inspiration for those like me in today's RAF and hopefully those who will follow in our footsteps in tomorrow's RAF.

"Lest we forget".

FT/L Martin Wintermeyer - RAF

MEMORIES OF A DIFFERENT WORLD

Charles Gallagher

SOUTH AFRICA

Self, Cadet at Cambridge University, 1942

February 1943 – the Germans had failed to take Moscow and turned their armies south to the Russian oilfields. Japan had been checked at Midway and Italy wanted peace. Britain no longer stood alone and Bing Crosby sang "White Christmas".

The year dawned bright and cold as several hundred 19 year old air crew cadets boarded the S.S. Strathmore bound for South Africa and Rhodesia, on the Empire Air Training Scheme. Most of us had never been as far as the Isle of Wight. Distant memories come tumbling down the years as over the next five weeks we zigzagged as part of a major troop convoy across the Atlantic to avoid the U-boats. Part of the convoy separated east to support the 1st Army in North Africa while we sailed on south, with a number of troop ships whose final destination was India.

On deck the fascination and sight of never ending water, an occasional navy Destroyer racing in from its protecting screen. Approaching the tropics, dolphins appeared displaying their dazzling mastery of the sea. All new and fascinating – a chance

1

to reflect on a journey which only seemed like yesterday from University life into the RAF.

Over the years, often the question, "Why was the Royal Air Force your first choice?"

Age certainly determined much of the answer. For a generation of young men who were leaving School and the Universities during and after that long hot and momentous summer of 1940 we had watched another generation only just before us save our Country against desperate odds in the skies over England – the Battle of Britain.

The Aircrew uniform had become our objective, the young men who wore it our inspiration.

Back to reality on board ship. A rigid routine of physical fitness, a part of everyday RAF life in every weather. As the weather warmed solo whist took over during off duty hours in the evening.

Below deck the scene was less romantic but more challenging. The small number of salt water showers and loos required skills, experience and above all endurance at exceptional levels to get in and at the mutually required time.

Similar personal qualities enabled us to get a little sleep after hanging our hammocks at night in limited space and later in tropical heat. At the Mess tables food was good and sufficient. However, in the tropics you learned never to accept an offer of salt from the cook as he hovered above and behind you ladling mealies into your porridge bowl. Should you ask for it, inclining his head forward you got it straight and accurately into your bowl without the help of his spoon!

Political lectures on the situation in South Africa put us in the picture on Afrikaner politics. Segregation, although not becoming official apartheid until after the war, was strictly in place at the time. A two day call at Freetown holds special memories. On the second evening as the light faded the sound of a lone Piper from another ship came across the water.

Singing followed as thousands of troops from ship after ship took up the old songs from home – emotionally deeply moving on a hot still night in Africa.

One morning in the early dawn we were woken by the silence of the engines and stillness of the ship. Hurrying on deck we were fascinated to see scores of seals looking up at us, apparently as interested in our arrival at Cape Town as we in their reception.

As I recall, we sailed two days later, arriving on a glorious morning at Durban, the city skyline standing proud, white and tall.

The "Lady in White" as she became known to the Services welcomed our convoy in as always standing and singing through a megaphone on the quay. By chance, years later, I saw her obituary in the Telegraph and her award of the British Empire Medal.

Africa at last – we were shipped in lorries to the Imperial transit camp at Clarewood some eight miles out of Durban. About ten days here and memorable for its loos and the manner of their construction. The loos consisted of a long concrete "shed" on a slight slope with three concrete and functional blocks where some 15 men could and did sit reasonably spaced on each, back to back to 15 others. A stream of adequate strength ran underneath. The architect had ensured a delightful privacy by designing a low screen between each group of 30 men.

A full house as it always was before morning parade was interesting and occasionally exciting in the lower group areas when lighted newspapers were sent downstream by cadets from higher up.

On a day's Leave two of us decided to try our luck on getting in to Durban. After a while a car stopped, the driver, forty-ish and alone beckoned us into the back seat. We jumped in murmuring our thanks and waited. Several minutes of total silence and then

3

suddenly a long assault on the British Empire and in particular those who had built it. Another uncomfortable silence followed and then for the first time looking at us – "you boys won't have transport so you can have my car for the day – bring it back by 6pm to my office where we are going now" – exactly how it happened.

I remember little of the day or the legalities of the car but very clearly the scene of my first encounter with an Afrikaner and the value of those lectures sailing south. We called on the famous Durban zoo where my main memory was of a "friend" who popped a handful of harmless grass snakes, harmless as I discovered later, inside my shirt while looking at a very different kind of snake at the time.

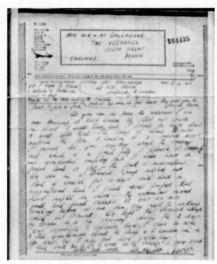

Airgraph

Mum & Dad kept all letters from South Africa during the war, and from India and Bermuda afterwards. Reading the first

Airgraph I wrote home from South Africa I see that my letter was dated 8th April and arrived home May 1st.

Leaving Clarewood we arrived at 48 Air School East London after a two day train journey through country I wrote at the time as "impossible to describe". Sixty seven years later I will say that the Drakensberg Mountains must frame some of the world's most beautiful country.

Our Camp was just outside East London – an attractive seaside resort. The first two weeks being spent under Canvas – our duties largely "Fatigues" – the least attractive job in the RAF.

Coming from war time rationing and shortages in the UK the quality and quantity of everything in the shops and restaurants was amazing. So far from the theatre of war – not surprising.

Our work at 48 Air School was to give us the ground preparation over 8 weeks on Navigation, Bombing, and Gunnery that we would later need in the air.

South Africa was of course at war – her 6th Division and Airforce fighting in the north and her air fields a base, as in Canada, for the Empire Air Training Scheme.

Our Course was due to start 3 weeks later in May – strange to think early winter!

Incredibly we got 10 days leave and two of us left for a farm on the High Veld the following evening.

Local farmers generously left invitations to their farms on the information board in the Mess. After a day on the beach in glorious weather we arrived at our first destination, a small village Sterkstrumm, 4000 ft. up on the High Veld, and were woken around 5am to the sound of crashing branches and trees falling under a weight of snow.

Mr Larter, a third generation English farmer, welcomed us at the little station and drove us out to the small village of Dordrecht, some mile or so from his farm. Almost immediately he told us that for our 10 days we could have a truck, a shot gun and a rifle as he was sure we would want "to get after the geese, duck and guinea fowl that flew in at this time of the year!"

Laurison Farm, May 1943, 7 days leave

Mr and Mrs Larter and their farm hands were wonderful hosts, giving us a tremendous week, but we found that for "getting after the guinea fowl" it was incredibly difficult to get near enough for a shot due to their extraordinary ability to outrun not only us but anything that moved over those wide open plains.

On returning to East London we began our Course working 08:00 – 12:00 and 13:00 – 16:00 hrs. A brief account of time in East London is from memory and where there are shadows I have Airgraphs.

In our off duty time we walked a great deal, boated on the Buffalo River invariably attended by large numbers of excited and chattering monkeys who were clearly amused by our presence.

We averaged three games of rugby a week – Airgraph footnote "I never felt fitter in my life – winter weather warm days and cool evenings." A dinner party every weekend at a hotel in East London became a delightful routine.

Letters from some of the old crowd at Blundells and Cambridge began to arrive in early June from various parts of the world – a great and super surprise. As we approached our exams we worked pretty hard and often until midnight while during the day a bulldog

6

joined our lectures – we felt Churchill had arrived!
July 1ˢᵗ exam results – PASSED!

A passing out parade – a superb celebration dinner.

Followed by private parties.

What a wonderful life!

A posting to our flying school followed immediately. Two of us caught the night train to Cape Town on the 6ᵗʰ July and on to 66 Air School at Young's Field only to find that the Posting had been changed to 45 Air School Oudtshoorn. However taking every advantage of the situation we had an unforgettable four days in Cape Town. Particularly memorable while walking down Adderley

Street on the Sunday morning in our "Blues" a chauffeur driven Rolls Royce with a little old lady in the back stopped alongside. "Would you boys like and have the time to jump in and see a bit of Cape Town and the coastal route round Camps Bay and Haupts Bay – a very beautiful area?" In less than 100th of a second two air crew cadets – the lowest form of life in the RAF – decided that they had both the time and an urgent wish to accept her invitation.

After a superb drive and trying desperately to thank her adequately – again the little voice "As you don't know Cape Town you may have little to do this evening. Would you care to come to a little party at my house if I could give one?"

In less time than before we assured her that we deeply cared – a day in a lifetime! I remember little more accept that the Party was not little, the house was "jainormous" and her name was – Rothschild.

Back at camp I feel our explanations to the Adjutant on exactly where we had been over part of those 4 days must have been a little sketchy but we got away with it.

On arriving at 45 Air School Oudtshoorn, a small country town, we found ourselves in the Little Karoo – a largely desert area and centre of the old ostrich trade in Victorian times when their feathers were greatly favoured by ladies for their hats. The Little Karoo led into the Great Karoo – the whole area surrounded on the coastal side by the 5000 ft. range of Outeniqua Mountains and to the north the 10,000 ft. Schwartzberg Mountains.

Cut into the hills the sign of the Osava Branva, flaming torches inside ox wagon wheels carved in white stone – a very small Afrikaner minority anti-British movement. However we didn't walk back to camp alone! At this point September and early summer we changed from Blues into Khaki. Four months at flying school was a splendid mix of hard work and off duty interests, enjoyment and fun. Flying or lectures started daily at 07:30 hrs. and from early

September at 05:00 hrs. – night flying twice a week. Our navigation training was in Ansons – Bombing and Gunnery in Oxfords.

Once a week on Fridays we left camp at 04:00hrs for 61 Air School George to do Gunnery practice on Oxfords. This was a glorious drive through mountainous country with an occasional view of a leopard.

Sadly two young South African cadets on our course were killed on a navigation training flight just behind us as we crossed a mountain area where Berg winds (strong air currents) caused their aircraft to crash.

Off duty we visited the world famous Kango Caves – a fantastic sight of stalactites and stalagmites. Every weekend we took a taxi (taxis) through the Outeniqua Mountains to the beautiful little coastal resort of Mossel Bay.

We slept sometimes in a hotel, occasionally on the beach, wonderful food, massive appetites, and a marvellous two day relaxation from the other five days.

A local man showed us round a garden he had cut into a part of the cliffs – quite incredible. Miniature houses, bridges, garden seats and a little shed with a dozen or so small deer. A very small blue grey – a Bluebuck – generously changed to RAFbuck as a compliment to the RAF. It was very beautiful and cleverly done.

The summer having arrived – it was very hot and we were starting to get some cricket – the first since Cambridge.

In those days donkey derbies were popular in South Africa. I put half a crown on a donkey that ran backwards and have never put anything on anything since!

As exams approached tension undoubtedly grew amongst all of us. In the final 6 weeks we had eleven exams. Over the 24 weeks at the two Air Schools, and having come thousands of miles to do it, failure was not an option.

November 15th – PASSED!

Celebration is a massive understatement for the events that followed.

Passing Out Parade and our promotion to Sergeant as qualified Navigator/Bomb Aimers.

Pay 7 shillings & sixpence per day advanced to 13 shillings & sixpence per day. We were rich!

A wonderful Dinner Party followed at an Oudtshoorn Hotel. Many more private Parties in town.

Again what a wonderful life!

Nine of us volunteered for a five week Reconnaissance Course at our Gunnery School 61 Air School George which would qualify us for either Bomber Command or Coastal Command depending on need when we got home. George was a beautiful little coastal resort, now these many years later a large tourist attraction. We had five successful and happy weeks.

We left George by train just after Christmas on the fabulous little railway line winding up and up and over the Outeniqua Mountains – people often leaving the train to catch it again higher up!

Our destination Durban – we once again experienced the glory of the Drakensberg Range sitting out the evening sunsets on little platforms between the carriages and contemplating life comfortably through the glass of a Lion beer.

As we left Durban on the Arundel Castle a dramatic memory – several hundred Topees, a part of our tropical kit issue and never used, were thrown as one into the harbour to a background of cheering. An expensive operation but we could never understand why we had been issued with them.

We sailed north ending with a fascinating passage up the Suez Canal watching Royal Marines training their powerful hoses on the endless vendors of every type and description who tried to board the ship to sell their wares.

The light cruiser Belfast, now moored at London Bridge, picked us up at Port Said and escorted us home.

How many of the boys who sailed south on the Strathmore just a year before share these memories today – 2014?

HMS Belfast 1939-Wartime Colours

BOMBER COMMAND TRAINING

January 1944. On a cold, bleak January day after five months initial training at Cambridge University Air Squadron in 1942 and a year's flying training in South Africa in the following year it was the last day of a week's disembarkation leave on returning to the UK.

Life at almost twenty looked to be on track.

Objective, an Operational Squadron within the year.

First to an assembly point at the Queens' Hotel at Harrogate in Yorkshire.

The following morning, weather freezing, a cross-country run was the order of the day and fortunately we moved off before actually freezing into the ground – 10 days back from South Africa in mid-summer to Yorkshire in mid-winter.

First a posting to an Advanced Flying Unit at Millom in Cumberland followed immediately – three weeks acclimatisation flying on navigation and bombing conditions in Europe.

STANTON HARCOURT

A posting to an Operational Training Unit at Stanton Harcourt, a satellite station to Abingdon in the Cotswolds followed.

We flew Whitley two-engine bombers during our seven week Course through the summer. Training was based on learning to fly the Whitley as a crew, mostly navigation, bombing, and an introduction to defensive Combat flying – a Spitfire joined us from a local fighter station. Corkscrewing (violent evasive action) would follow, always an interesting and eventful couple of hours!

It was here that we "Crewed-up" – the most memorable day in our entire training. On the first day we were assembled in a large room, pilots, navigators, bomb-aimers, wireless operators, flight engineers and gunners – around 84 men, 12 crews as I recall. We were then left alone, told to "mix" and decide ourselves who we wanted to fly with, seemingly an extraordinary method of selection. It turned out to be the perfect way, a Bomber Crew depending totally on each other for their effectiveness and survival, both decided largely by the choices made gave a remarkable focus to the day!

For example, later on the Squadron the flight engineer would be responsible for control of the fuel, some 2,000 gallons positioned above 12,000 lbs. of high explosives and / or incendiaries – a useful idea to get his decisions right! Jim Portwood and I had been friends from when we met up on the Arundel Castle troopship coming home from South Africa – we were both trained and qualified Navigators and as I had also trained as a Bomb

Aimer it enabled us to form an immediate partnership of Navigator and Bomb Aimer respectively.

We went looking for a Pilot, a useful thing to have, and we quickly found Flight Lieutenant "Mac" Macfarlane, whom we discovered had way above average flying hours and experience as a Pilot at this stage, having qualified at an American air base, Gunter's Field in Alabama, and stayed on for a further year to train others. We talked our training records fully, liked each other, asked him if he would like us to join him – he said he would and we now had part of a team including a Skipper. During the rest of the day we found two Gunners Jack Taylerson mid upper turret and Jock Davidson tail-gunner on his second Tour (he had already done 30 "Ops" on his first Tour so now had only 20 to do with us on his second). On our twenty-first Operation Nic Nicholson joined us for the final 10 trips of our Tour. Shep Shepperd came in as our Wireless Operator who at 27 years we regarded as very old indeed, an ex ground-crew operator serving in Burma who came home and re-mustered to Aircrew. Finally our Flight Engineer, little Jock Farquhar – we had a crew, 8 life-long friends, Mac & I to this day.

We were fortunate to get an experienced rear-gunner on his second tour for our first twenty operations and to have him replaced by another excellent gunner, Nic Nicholson, on our twenty first trip.

MEMORIES OF STANTON HARCOURT

To our surprise and delight we found on arrival that only a small wood stood between the site of our billets and the village pub fostering an exceptional and immediate relationship between the landlord of the Fox and ourselves.

A glorious summer day and a small American aircraft had buzzed around the airfield several times while we sat on the grass waiting to go up on a training flight. Finally it landed, out got two American Officers, pulling out cigars, and to our amazement lighting them up – a map followed, a long look, a shrug – they saw us and walked across "Say guys – can you tell us where we are?" We told them and to our delight "Shucks – missed it again" – confirming our assessment which at that time we held of American navigation. We never saw them again.

I have long forgotten how I acquired her, but it was here that a young sheepdog puppy became mine and it was necessary to persuade the Crew that she would be an asset if she joined us in our nissan hut. The look of doubt on their faces I remember to this day. Anything falling from a bed, mostly socks, were instantly chewed and shredded. Goodwill amongst the Crew went into free-fall. I got a day's leave and Sarie arrived home at South Brent on Dartmoor to become a wonderful member of our family for many years to come. Her name Sarie came from an Afrikaner song 'Sarie Marais' which we had sung over many a pint in South Africa.

MARSTON MOOR

It was now time to learn to fly the 4-engine Halifax, our future operational aircraft as a Crew. Our posting to a Heavy Conversion unit came and we arrived at Marston Moor near York. It was here General Fairfax routed the Royalist army under Prince Rupert during the civil war some 300 years earlier. Our first view of the Halifax close up – we liked it and in the coming months we came to love it. Initially, practice take offs and landings (circuits and bumps) were the priority training. Mac took some heavy flak and wise-cracks for some of the early landings. The Crew's consensus being that it must feel similar to being shot down. Mac was not amused! All previous training now continued with increasing emphasis on defence against fighter attack.

MEMORIES OF MARSTON MOOR

The Crew was walking back from the airfield to our quarters one late September afternoon when we came across half a dozen or so men and girls working in a cornfield. I trust we had no thoughts of supper when we offered our help but some two hours later that was what they offered us.

While at Marston Moor several wonderful supper parties followed with Farmer Smith, his delightful wife and three unquestionably delightful daughters of around our age. The table would be loaded with a fantastic display of food, some rarely seen due to wartime rations. When supper ended the girls asked if we would like to join them in some old Yorkshire songs – a piano would come out and the old farmhouse shook as we all joined in – a memory that will never fade and hopefully of family values that will always stand.

Tapestry

At a Squadron Association reunion many years after the war a service was held in the RAF chapel in York Minster to dedicate the Embroidery worked by the wives of our Crew to lie under the Book of Remembrance which records the 20,000 Air Crew killed who flew from the Yorkshire airfields during the war. A huge complement to our wives for only the finest work was ever accepted by the Minster.

Bomber Command lost a total of 55,573 killed, around 8,500 wounded, around 10,000 Prisoners of War out of a total of 125,000 during the war.

Mrs Smith, who by now was over 90 years old, to our great delight, attended that service.

BOMBER COMMAND
76 SQUADRON 4 GROUP
HOLME-ON-SPALDING MOOR
VALE OF YORK

One morning in November 1944 our posting to an Operational Squadron arrived. We had waited a long time. It was surely a tribute to our training that memory tells of just another day except for one difference, our colleagues and friends were now Operational Air Crews and the Ground Crews to whom we came to owe so massive a debt.

We found ourselves on 76 Halifax Squadron, founded in 1916 during the Royal Flying Corps days of World War I.

In the summer of 1944 the Squadron was based some 15 miles south of York near the village of Holme-on-Spalding Moor in the Vale of York.

Memories of that winter long ago vary between the serious, the ridiculous and the fun. The combination of the three at the average age of 20 years created the perfect balance to form six of the most memorable months of our lives.

First let's have a glance at a bit of the fun and ridiculous.

THE SKIPPER – Mac was a great Pilot and Skipper – exceptional, but his waterworks control was not in the same category, especially on a long trip. However, superstition was widespread and came to the rescue. For example, Jim had a photo of his girlfriend which he moved to a special pocket on "Ops". I wore pyjamas under my flying kit and Jack, most fortunately for Mac, would only fly on "ops" starting with a full bottle of milk.

Once empty it would be passed as quickly as possible to Mac should an overflow emergency occur.

Detail is fortunately not required as the family has heard this story over the supper table several times, invariably at the request of the grandchildren. May I leave it that Mac's technique left much to be desired but in fairness the combination of a milk bottle, probably considerable turbulence, and a hostile audience below were never favourable to a steady hand, or quick judgement. Shep's position almost directly below him enabled the rest of us to have huge fun at the expense of both of them!

SHEP – Shep had been having trouble with his teeth and coupled with constant air sickness problems decided to change them for a new set.

Decision taken: teeth out: new ones installed: his pride and joy, assured us he was a new man. We assured him that this was tremendous news for us all!

Some two weeks later somewhere over Holland he was bailing out "Window" – thousands of metalized foil strips to jam the German radar.

It was turbulent and out went the "Window" along with his supper and teeth. For Shep it was now a very personal war – "Somebody in that B…y Third Reich is wearing my teeth". There was a time when Jim and I began to be seriously concerned by how white he had begun to look on "Ops". During the long periods maintaining his radio silence watch he would sit with his curtains drawn so we decided to have a look an hour or two into the trip. Behind the curtain, white as a sheet, he was staring at an open paperback dispensing a level of horror that would terrify anyone – a big laugh when we got home.

A CHANGE IN VENUE

My 21st Birthday in February – an evening in York planned – but it was not to be. At 13.25 the Log Book recalls on that day the Crew were airborne to Kamen, an oil refinery just east of the Ruhr.

Given a choice for your 21st, a date with one of the most beautiful cities in the world or a few minutes over an oil refinery in Germany – but options there were none!

A NIGHT IN THE CELLS

An unexpected 48 hours leave between Operations saw the Crew on station transport heading for York around 18.00 hrs. on a winter's evening in 1944 and on to our various homes – mine a Dartmoor vicarage in South Brent in Devon.

My train turned out to end it's life for the night at Totnes, a beautiful little country town I had known so well as a boy as "Toters" but not welcome on a wintry night in the early hours before dawn.

Who should be standing on an almost empty platform but a policeman for no apparent reason. He asked me if I had anywhere to sleep as the next stopping train was several hours away. If not I would be welcome in his station cells and transport would be arranged there and back. I assured him I thought it a most generous offer, would be delighted to accept, and it might be possible to enter me on the station register as a guest, so avoiding a criminal record.

Despite the hour an interesting and enjoyable night followed. About 7am I had arrived at Brent and within 10 minutes I was climbing through the kitchen window which had been left open for me. A long chat with Mum and Dad sitting on their bed and then down for breakfast in another world from just two nights ago. Not a single bark from Sarie – how amazingly they always know when its family.

COMMISSIONED

With about half our Tour completed Jim and I were commissioned from Flight Sergeants to Pilot Officers and were given Leave to get our new uniforms from Gieves, the Service tailors in London.

Our unofficial objective was to try and get a sight of a "Flying Bomb" (doodle bugs) but sadly we were unlucky.

I asked Mac to contribute four particular memories – two training and two operational flights.

TRAINING FLIGHTS

Mac writes "I do remember an early daylight cross-country navigational training flight working the aircraft up. We overhauled a USAF B17 Flying Fortress on a similar mission in our Halifax MkIII capable of 200 knots.

"We sailed past the B17 which was only doing about 170 knots with both our port engines feathered (cut), with the Crew making appropriate friendly gestures out of the windows to the Crew of the B17. Their response came from their Skipper who over the RT was heard to say "Yeah, yeah, yeah!"

Mac writes again "I'd like to tell you about an incident that happened at Holme-on-Spalding-Moor.

"On 27th November 1944 when we were engaged on a practice bombing detail, a regular occurrence on 76 Squadron, we assembled at our aircraft in the afternoon about 14.00 hrs, if my memory is correct, took our positions in the aircraft and started her up. We were given permission to taxi to the take-off runway, in this case taking off to the west – the short runway crossing the main runway some distance along its length. This runway was bordered by a stretch of woodland some 100 yds. to our right side.

"We arrived at the take-off point and received a green light from the ACP truck – the chap in charge of the runway – and it was his duty to see that the runway was clear of all traffic.

"We started our roll, opening the throttles to maximum, we gained speed steadily and as we approached the intersection of the 2 runways Charles who was acting as co-pilot said 'Look' and pointing out of his starboard window we saw a small car with a canvas roof being driven along the main runway and would appear to reach the intersection at the same time as we would.

"There was no time to slow down as we already were doing 90 knots but still not up to flying speed.

"To try and swing the aircraft was out of the question and if we hit this car there would be a catastrophe of enormous proportions. I did the only thing possible and that was to push the control column hard forward and then back and try to bounce the machine over the car. That is what happened – the oleo legs of the under-carriage being compressed when I pushed the column forward and on pulling back they assisted the machine to leap in the air and we plonked back down on the runway still gathering speed. As we felt nothing untoward and by now the rest of the Crew were asking questions, I checked with the Rear Gunner about this car and he said it was still driving along the other runway. It's canvas hood was off to one side but the car seemed intact. We felt relieved and as we now had flying speed we climbed away to carry out our detail.

"We rather forgot about this incident but on our return and having parked the aircraft, we were met by the station commander Group Capt. Pelly-Fry and all hell was let loose. The incident had been seen naturally by Flying Control. The problem was that the car in question eventually came off the main runway onto the grass and came to a halt. On investigation they found an elderly gentleman inside – dead. There was an immediate court of enquiry and it was discovered that the man in the car was an elderly farmer who farmed to the north of the aerodrome and he had a brother who farmed on the south side of the airfield and the main runway ran between the two farms.

"The farmer from the north side found it very convenient to drive through the woodland onto this "fine new road" which took him straight to his brother's farm out through the airfield boundary on the south side. So much for security of the airfield!

"In addition the driver of the car was severely deaf and never heard the aircraft taking off. We were successful in jumping over the car but the slipstream from the propellers was so great that it tore the canvas roof off – the two bolts holding the crane of the hood were old and rusty and had been snapped off and the metal bar hit the old boy on his temple and unfortunately killed him, and apparently his foot did not come off the throttle for some time until eventually he came to rest on the grass.

"His brother said he had been using that "nice new road" for some time and no one had noticed. After this incident I carried a couple of pilot instruction manuals written in English of two German aircraft, the JU88 and the ME110, on the premise that if German airfields were similar to ours, and I had to bail out over Germany I might have a go at flying home rather than walking!

"As a Crew we were rather saddened by this accident and were left off duty for a few days, and then the Squadron doctor, Doctor Marix, got hold of me, told me I'd been through a harrowing time and insisted that I take the "night night" tablets he produced to knock me out and get a good night's sleep.

"Well, I did, the next day I looked dreadful but eventually got to the NAAFI cafeteria, met the boys and got in line for a cup of tea and smoked what in those days was a drag on my Sunripe cigarette. On that same day, one of the pretty WAAF girls pointed me out to her companion that I was the brave pilot involved in that nasty accident from the day before. And who did that new companion become – my future wife Marian. The ways of women!!!!!"

Training can also be memorable!
Mac won't admit it but that was a hell of a piece of flying!

OPERATIONAL TOUR

November 30th 1944 – My log book records our first Operation.

Date	Hour	Aircraft	Target	Flying Times	
				Day	Night
30/11/44	16.45	MPK – X	Duisburg		5.50 hrs.

The industrial heart of Germany – the Ruhr – known to thousands of Aircrew as "Happy Valley", one of the most heavily defended areas in Germany.

The targets were generally the nearest to home averaging between 5.50hrs and 6.50hrs. – hopefully!

And so at Duisburg almost 70 years ago it began. That night we became a Crew; that night we discovered the difference between an evening in a Yorkshire pub and the next in the night skies over Germany.

Battle Orders

"We're on Tonight."

Target guessing immediately, knowing well that answers were under lock and key until Briefing.

A guard stood at the entry to the Briefing Room. On our first "Op" memorable I suppose as we realized that at last it was for real. The Guard coming to attention announced the arrival of the Commanding Officer bringing us all to our feet.

On a maximum effort the Squadron put up around 25 aircraft. Tension increased as the target was revealed along with route in, route out, type of bomb load, fuel load, German defences along the route, with latest intelligence on flak, fighters, and the Met Forecast to and over the Target.

Reaction to the target defences was individual, barely audible, usually humorous, and always unrepeatable. As the Briefing closed we separated to our own groups, Pilots, Navigators, Bomb Aimers, etc., to finalize our own section planning.

All now depended on the time of take-off and during the severe wartime rationing bacon and eggs at supper were only available to Aircrew on "Ops" that night, or breakfast in the case of a daylight operation.

Until take off we still had to kit-up with flying clothing, silk and wool long-johns underneath – it being chilly at 18,000 feet and frequently down to minus 50 degrees. A call to the parachute room still to come to draw parachutes – one of the great fun memories before a trip to the Fatherland, endless 20 year old jokes such as "Did you pack this one?" to the WAAF handing it to you "God, no thanks – I'll be safer going down without one". You were lucky if it wasn't thrown at you. A great bunch of girls, many a laugh and perhaps even an ocasional tear.

Then into the truck and out to your aircraft.

Final pre-flight checks and a memory for the rest of your life – the sound, feel and smell of an entire fully loaded Bomber Squadron getting airborne for an operation.

I remember little of our first operation except of how it started.

A cold grey dusk lay across a silent Squadron when suddenly

a single engine coughed then stuttered into life signalling the start of the engine check – a gathering storm of sound as aircraft after aircraft started to run up its engines.

As I recall we stood about six in the order of take-off which enabled us to watch five other aircraft get airborne, turn onto the runway in use, pause for an intense moment, then with a surge of power, sound and speed roar down the runway and lift off at around 100 knots, our flying speed. A spectacular and exhilarating sight. How do I describe how it felt? Clearly the adrenalin was running high. The combination of two years of intensive and successful training coupled with the formation of a Crew we had ourselves selected enabled us to meet this moment – we had confidence in each other.

After seventy years it is interesting to remember that when Operational we carried up to 2,000 gallons of fuel positioned in the aircraft just above 12,000 lbs. of high explosives.

Thinking back on what had the most impact on my overall feelings during our Operational Tour my thoughts go back to that day in 1944 at our Operational Training Unit at Stanton Harcourt which I described earlier where we "crewed up" as the most memorable day of our training. As you know we were left alone, told to "mix" and decide ourselves who we wanted to fly with. We were astounded for it was so unexpected a method of selection. We were not to be placed in a Crew but to create our own. The choices made would probably decide our survival and depend heavily on Comradeship and a sense of Humour creating the necessary balance to pressures and their resulting distractions. We made the right choices, had a great collective sense of humour and we became I believe a mentally strong, positive and effective Operational Crew, and at times a very fortunate one – we always came back!

Endless wonderful opportunities for the sense of humour to come in to play and release the tensions and pressures. The selection method had been fully vindicated.

OPERATIONAL FLIGHTS

Mac writes about a February 1945 night operation.

A Little Tale Of How To Be Frightened

"This afternoon we were briefed to attack an oil target called Wanneeikel, just to the north and east of Essen in the middle of the Ruhr. It was not the target the railway marshalling yards that got us frightened, but the getting there!

"We were briefed to fly straight to the Yorkshire coast from our bases around York, mostly 4 Group – about 240 aircraft, were to fly in close formation and not to fly above 500 ft. over the North Sea in order to keep below a diversion Mandrelling screen being used for the operation.

"Did I hear someone say "What's a Mandrelling screen?" – Well it is an electronic screen created by a special unit of aircraft from 100 Group to confuse the German radar and also when required to listen to radio broadcasts from German controllers and to intervene on the same frequency by giving amended instructions to upset the Luftwaffe pilots. Most of our German speakers were Jewish and had they fallen into German hands they would have been shot instantly.

"The route out was due east for the region of Schleswig Holstein, just south of the Danish border and in the area of the Kiel Canal. Flight briefing had detailed that the weather forecast for the North Sea crossing was not good with poor visibility but cheerfully said that the weather would improve the further east we went and would be clear for the target area which after all was why we were going.

"The briefing required us to maintain low level until about 50 miles from the German coast then climb rapidly to 18,000 ft. over

29

the coast. There would be a turning point to take us south to the target area.

"Pathfinder flares would mark the target and aiming point. We set off about 20:00 hrs heading east, soon crossing the Yorkshire coast, all aircraft buzzing across the sea like a swarm of bees.

"We were below cloud and could make out shapes of aircraft around us, then suddenly we were in cloud, thick stuff, couldn't see a thing. Everybody obviously was now flying on instruments and then we all put our navigation lights on. Remember we had barely 500 ft. below us and not being allowed above 500 ft. most aircraft were flying nearer to 400 ft.

"In radio silence with me concentrating on my instruments the rest of the Crew with eyes on stalks stared out of the windows into the pitch black of flying in cloud at night. Navigation lights from other bombers would appear eerily out of the fog and disappear to be replaced by another on our other side, when one aircraft came over the top of us and its propellers nearly took off the astrodome on the top of our aircraft. We had no idea of what other bombers were below us in the darkness other than the sea some 400ft below.

"All of a sudden another aircraft appeared out of the gloom immediately above us; only inches away so close we heard the noise of its engines before we saw anything. We were all electrified and immediately said to Jack, our mid-upper Gunner –

"Did you not see that coming?"

"What coming?" replied Jack.

"That aircraft that nearly took the roof off" –

"Naw," said Jack. "I was blowing me nose" he said in his inimitable Lancashire accent.

"Jack received a hurl of abuse across the intercom and was ordered under no circumstance to blow his nose again. And so we progressed across the North Sea all our senses completely on edge expecting disaster to occur at any moment, until on dead reckoning Jim our Navigator told us the time had come to climb. Still in cloud and still very anxious about watching for other aircraft we climbed to 18,000ft. We all heaved a huge sigh of relief when we emerged from the cloud and came out on top to find we were nearly over land on the Dutch coast.

"Until that point Jim had little opportunity to fix our position using the astrodome and when at last he did, he calculated that the estimated Met Wind speeds from the operational briefing were not correct and that we had ended up far too far to the east of our target – Jim gave us a reciprocal heading to take us south west to the target. From a distance we eventually saw some target flares to the north and turned then north and east to take us as close to the target as we could. Charlie got us lined up to bomb them which we did. This time we crossed the target uneventfully and swiftly turned for home – to carry on would have taken us into the heavily defended Hamburg area. At this time of the war although the threat of German night-fighters had waned the flak defences around major German cities were at their height with more than two million anti-aircraft guns many of which were now tied to radar based installations. Germany was still a very hostile place to be in an aircraft lumbering along at 200 knots.

"Flying in and out of cloud on the way home with little time for astro-fixes Charles reckoned we were near Copenhagen – I did not think so but we might well have been getting over the Baltic as Schleswig Holstein was quite narrow at that point. In my view the planning of the operation was dangerous with so much low flying in cloud on the out bound leg with the danger of collision being so high, the forecast winds were all wrong which would mean that many less experienced crews would end up in the wrong place, quite frankly it was a hopeless operation and a waste of time which would have undoubtedly cost lives. If there were any casualties, and I'm sure aircraft were lost through hitting each other. Any aircraft which had got away with being merely damaged would have been in serious trouble over the North Sea that night. The idea of trying to land a damaged machine in the North Sea and surviving would stretch anyone's imagination, especially in the month of February with water temperatures so low. We got home safely and lived to fly another day! However, I'm sure there were those who did not"

Mac writes again,

"March 25th, 1945 – Time 07.00 hrs.

"The routine was pretty much the same for every operation. There was a knock on the door.

"A sergeant put his head round the door and said "Sorry to disturb you Sir. You are all requested to report to the Briefing Room by 07:30 hrs. Urgent." Slammed the door shut and we started another day at Holme-On-Spalding Moor. 07:30 hrs saw a pretty sleepy-eyed Crew collecting outside the Briefing Room. A glance at the Log Book showed three Operations in the previous four days. A bit of justification for the bleary eyes! Still wondering why the emergency – we soon found out.

"The Winco got up and apologized for the early call but Headquarters had asked for the Group to bomb Osnabruck, a German communications Rail Centre. And so the Briefing proceeded along the usual lines of route in and route out, amount and type of bomb load, fuel load, information on anti-aircraft defences and possible fighter defence, weather to be expected, and that on this occasion the entire Squadron would be led by Flight Lieutenant Macfarlane and his Crew.

"In addition, there would be an extra crew member with us, a young wireless operator of only nineteen who three weeks before when returning from his second trip, had been shot down by a JU88 intruder whilst coming in to land at Holme.

"This young lad had to bail out from about 800 ft. and was rather shaken up by the experience but had now had three weeks off "Ops" to get over it and was now going out with an experienced Crew and as the Winco said "You'll be alright – nothing ever happens to Mac and his Crew".

"We were given breakfast, then out to our aircraft, but instead of our usual beloved aircraft "Q-Queenie" which was being given an engineering check, we were given "X-XRAY" a MkIII Halifax and the oldest aircraft on the Squadron, which had done 100 "Ops".

"It also had a mid-under Gunner position but on this trip we did not have a mid-under gunner with us but not to worry we got on board and ran through our pre-flight checks and then waited for the "off", started the engines, got clearance to taxi and being the lead aircraft "X" was soon airborne with the rest of the Squadron joining and other Squadrons adding to their numbers until we had over one hundred heading for Germany in bright sunshine.

"At cruising height, 18,000 ft. we levelled off and then we were confronted by an American Bomber Group returning home at our height. There was the customary polite waving and hand gestures exchanged as we passed each other.

"We went to the right, they went to their right and we avoided any trouble, and settled down and headed towards the Fatherland again. It was a beautiful day and we got all the way to the target with no resistance from the Germans.

"We could easily see Osnabruck halfway between Dortmund and Hamburg as Bomb-aimer Charles got busy with the run up to the target. Normally curtains were used at night but on this flight disregarded as it was a daylight raid. So far the flak was light and we, in the lead, were now under the control of our Bomb

Aimer with his "left left – hold it there – keep it steady – right – hold it steady – steady – Bombs Gone" as recorded by Charles.

"At that instant there was an almighty explosion right under the aircraft from a heavy shell – the Halifax was thrown violently up in the air and the heavy smell of cordite and a dreadful clanging noise of shrapnel passing through the aircraft.

"For a few seconds I wrestled with the controls. After what seemed an eternity I shouted "It's alright, I've got it" – meaning I had got the aircraft under control – an expression often used in training as I was an ex-instructor and followed procedure, but the rest of the Crew interpreted it as "Oh Christ, I've copped it", or something perhaps not so polite.

"The next thing we saw was our young wireless operator passenger ashen faced putting on his parachute and trying to open the pilot's escape exit in blind panic. I bent down and pulled him up by his collar and shouted "It's OK – we're still flying."

"By now we were flying out of the target area, still up front and settling down to assess the damage. A remarkable picture began to appear in the Bomb Aimer position. Charles had just turned away to re-set the bombs away switches in case of hang ups after reporting "Bombs Gone". As he turned back to his bomb site he found it had completely disappeared out through the top of his plastic nose cone and he was staring down through a large hole in the nose of the aircraft at Germany from 18,000 feet.

"At the same time, the Navigator who normally stood to watch the bombing run sat down after the explosion only to find where his head had been beside the de-icing tank through the side windscreen had come a large piece of shrapnel punching a hole right through the tank. For a fraction of a second Jim thought he was covered in blood but decided it was too cold for that.

"The biggest shock of all came to the Wireless Operator, Shep. Normally on the outward trip as he maintained radio silence he used to read western novels and believed that the bad guy in his novel was about to shoot the hero of the story when this shell exploded underneath the aircraft. Large amounts of shrapnel had passed up through the radio compartment taking out his window and half his radio set. Remarkably he survived without even a scratch although his western was shredded.

"Around the aircraft a picture of carnage began to appear.

"Our young passenger wireless operator's nerves had completely gone. It was decided to keep him busy by ordering him to try and put the destroyed radio back again while Shep was sent back with the engineer our temporary flight engineer Smithy to assess the damage in the rear of the aircraft. Smithy, our Engineer Leader, had replaced Jock on this one as he was ill.

"Meanwhile I found that the port outer engine had been severely damaged and was producing little power but fortunately had not caught fire. This was a major challenge for the Crew – a bomber flying out of the target area on three engines was a sitting duck in daylight for enemy fighters. To feather the engine was now a major decision to the survival of the aircraft and it's Crew. I guessed by varying the throttles that the engine was achieving some power, just enough to overcome possible drag if the propeller remained un-feathered (cut). Quickly I made the decision not to feather the engine thus avoiding the possibility of X-XRAY becoming fair game if spotted by an enemy fighter on the return trip.

"However, on only three serviceable engines the aircraft started to slip back through the squadron not helped by its age and that the aircraft around it needed to maintain the scheduled flying speed for the operation. At this point I radioed the stream of aircraft that we were on three engines and for the squadron to proceed home without X-XRAY.

"The flight engineer Smithy now told me that the centre bay area appeared to have suffered extensive damage behind the used seats in the take-off position. The unoccupied lower-mid gun position was completely destroyed with massive holes through the gun position and we were all very conscious that any gunner in that position would not have made it. Smithy's further investigations discovered that the "push pull rod" that controls the ailerons had been shot through and was broken meaning that the aircraft could only just turn and that the elevator rod was 75% cut – the rudder rod was also damaged. The undercarriage had also sustained heavy damage but as yet we the Crew had no idea if it was functioning. Smithy commenced to try and affect repairs to the control rods.

"Remarkably we were still flying.

"Meanwhile the mid and rear gunners had lost all intercom contact with the front of the aircraft because the wires had been cut, so it was agreed to substitute a light system should the aircraft be attacked.

"Later when Nic the rear-gunner was asked if he knew what was going on at the time of being hit by flak, he merely replied that he was a bit non-plussed and was all ready to bail out of the rear turret but as he waited and saw no shutes from a hastily departing Crew he decided things couldn't be too bad so stayed with the aircraft.

"And so we headed for home, getting further and further behind our squadron and the other bombers in the stream until we were eventually on our own flying over Germany and occupied Holland in broad daylight. I had managed to turn the aircraft in roughly the right direction by varying the power across the three remaining engines. Smithy had managed to lash together wire around the broken control rods to give us the ability to gently climb and descend and with wind howling through the various smashed parts of the fuselage we limped back to England, with our extra "bod" still trying to re-build the smashed radio shaking like a leaf. We eventually made it back to base and could speak to

Holme-on-Spalding Moor on a spare emergency H/F radio. Rather unsporting they told us to go to the emergency landing strip at Carnaby near Bridlington on the Yorkshire coast. Carnaby had one of the longest landing-strips in the country and was specifically there to help banged-up aircraft who were in trouble.

"Some surprises still awaited us. We now discovered we did not have any hydraulics to lower the landing gear, not that that was a trouble to us for as the Engineer removed the up-lock pins the heavy landing gear literally fell down and locked into position in the wings.

"At a safe height, I as Aircraft Commander then ordered the Crew to bail-out whilst I attempted to land the heavily damaged aircraft with no hydraulics, a dodgy undercarriage, on three engines and with only limited flight control. My Crew rather impolitely refused to bail-out and as I was to report years later "they were a mutinous Crew!"

"We came in successfully and landed alright but the aircraft's tyres were shredded, all three wheels. Boy was it knobbly for those in the crash positions in the middle of the aircraft! The aircraft came to a juddering halt. We clambered out, glad to be back home. Made it, piece of cake!

"It was then we saw the full extent of the damage to the mid-under gun position which had been wiped out – so it was a good thing no-one was in there. We walked slowly around X X-RAY looking at all the holes and thanked our lucky stars. We left our aircraft where it came to rest. The station supplied transport to take us back to Holme for a few well-earned beers.

"76 Squadron Engineering came to recover the aircraft but decided to leave it there as it was so heavily damaged – they just junked it.

"I recall that Marian, my wife in later years, who at the time was a young WAAF aircraft fitter on the Squadron, told me that when she and the C-Flight ground crew went out to salvage spare parts from "X XRAY" for other aircraft in the flight the only undamaged equipment they brought back from the aircraft was the fire-axe. Fortunately the only piece of equipment we didn't need to use that day!

"Marian and the ground crew counted 196 holes in the aircraft. And so on its 101st operation "X X-RAY" had made it home – just.

Marian, Mac's wife

"To the regular Crew's surprise next day the squadron's spare flight engineer leader, Smithy, who had flown with us had been watching the bombs drop when the aircraft was hit by flak. Having taken an inspection plate up to where you could look into the bomb bay, on his return he noticed that a tiny piece of flak had whipped through the inspection plate hole and given him a scratch on his forearm – you know the sort of scratch you might get when pruning roses. Nevertheless he put up a wound stripe on his uniform to commemorate the occasion to much bantering from the Crew.

"Sadly, as for our very young extra wireless operator crew member, he was still shaking like a leaf, and flatly refused to go on any more Operations. We asked him, but to no avail, and he was eventually assessed as not fit for duty, sent to the Correction Centre in Sheffield and stripped to the ranks being branded as LMF (Lack of Moral Fibre). Life could be very hard."

Earlier I described Mac as a great Pilot and Skipper – exceptional. He was. On that flight we had refused to bail out because we couldn't let him land her on his own in the condition she was in – no way.

THE AMERICAN 8TH AIR FORCE

Flying Fortresses & Liberators across south east England.

I must recall the visit we made to one of their airfields 73 years ago, as I write.

On the 6th December 1944 when returning from Soest in Central Germany, nearing the English south coast we had a signal diverting us to one of their airfields, Hethel in Norfolk, due to dense fog up north.

Landing at around 02.00 hrs we were welcomed warmly by their adjutant, a Major in the Officer's Mess. Due to the very short notice of our arrival he assured us he had briefed the cooks and said a prayer that the grub would be on the table quickly and in abundance, as he guessed we were probably hungry. Silently that prayer became mutual.

We had been away for around 8 hours over Central Germany with rather less than a handful of barley sugar – we were starving!

The cooks were brilliant, laughing, and wise-cracking at that hour of the night, very American and delightful – questions about Bomber Command – thoughtful and interesting. They provided a fantastic meal at incredibly short notice. God was listening. I believe we also played our part.

Sadly but understandably we saw very few American 8th Air Force aircrew as most were in bed and asleep but we saw them the following morning in great form. Comradeship and a wonderful sense of humour.

Before we rose from dinner the Major told us that a jeep and driver would be outside each Nissan hut first thing in the morning to take us to the PX. The PX was a general store full of chocolate, biscuits and all kinds of goodies that we hadn't seen for a long time – all in large quantities. You can imagine how we felt! We were invited to help ourselves to anything we wished to take as a gift back to Yorkshire.

I would like to write a couple of lines about the 8th for they were built on broadly the same structure as Bomber Command – comradeship, a wonderful sense of humour and the guts of men who had taken appalling casualties. The sacrifice they made.

By the autumn of 1941 France had been occupied for over a year. The Germans were just 11 miles away at Calais. We lived in daily expectation of possible invasion. In the circumstances morale was incredibly high.

When America came into the war on December 7th 1941 after the attack on Pearl Harbour by the Japanese I was still at school. We, the schoolboys of Blundells, were listening to the radio avidly officially or unofficially at any opportunity.

We spent our days going about our every day school activities – sport and work; many of us found it a matter of honour to even miss a lesson or two to get the latest news and prepared to then take the consequences!

As America entered the war, with her vast potential, a hopeful schoolboy dream became certain victory – whatever the time and however long it would take. Without the Americans Britain and the Allied Forces were facing likely defeat – with the Americans certain victory!

After 73 years, a long remarkable memory of welcome, comradeship, efficiency, generosity and good humour typical of the two Flying Commands.

"May I raise my 93 year old glass to the 8th American Air Force and the extraordinary memory of a wonderful night."

B-17 Flying Fortress

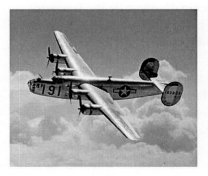

B-24 Liberator

STRANGE EVENTS – INCIDENT 1

Mac writes about a December 2nd 1944 operation to Hagen.

On this particular trip, which appears to be our third over Germany, the powers that be approached this target with a route giving the impression that it was going between the two towns of Dortmund and Cologne in order to fool the Luftwaffe night fighter command. Which one would be the target? Neither. The target was the Ruhr town of Hagen so there was a last minute course correction when the bomber stream turned south. Q-Queenie's navigator counted down the seconds to the point on Jim Portwood's chart and I turned the fully laden aircraft in the dark at the exact time with 504 other aircraft.

On such turns a pilot is trained to always look behind him, if he can, in the direction of the turn so that he does not collide with other aircraft. With so many aircraft turning at exactly the same time this is very chancy at the best of times. As I started to look right, while starting our turn, I distinctly heard a voice call urgently "look left, look left". I did, instantly, to find the dull red glow from a bomber's four engines directly to the left and about to ram into us. I immediately pulled back on the control column. We leaped into the air and another Halifax bomber whistled under us with about a foot to spare! Remember this was night time.

Then back on course again I asked the crew who had called out over the intercom to warn me of the approaching bomber! Each crew member called in; no-one had heard a warning call to 'look left', but me!

We bombed our designated target without further incident and turned for home. For some reason, we landed at Manston in Kent. I believe our base had fogged in.

We discussed our target with the intelligence debriefing team and talked quietly amongst the crew about the near accident and how lucky we were to avoid the two heavy laden bombers nearly colliding. The crew were convinced I must have imagined a voice warning me of impending danger. I replied that I did not see it that way, you see thinking about the warning voice on the return leg I was convinced that the warning came from a female and a voice I did not recognise.

When we returned to Holme-on-Spalding Moor the next day, we landed the aircraft at our usual airfield dispersal position. The crew next to us came running up to slap us on the back – they were the crew who nearly ran into us and they couldn't believe they missed us, their pilot said they were so close another coat of paint and he thought they were a 'goner'. The pilot said things had happened so quickly he'd not had time to manoeuvre his aircraft and was mightily relieved at my quick reactions. The question remains in my mind to this day; "who do you think might have warned us then?" Interesting, isn't it, if you believe in guardian angels?

STRANGE EVENTS – INCIDENT 2

Mac writes again, March 13th 1945 night operation to Wuppertal.

Following the incident of the car on the runway at Marston Moor while still training, other incidents come to mind, notably the one to Wuppertal in the Ruhr area of Germany. Wuppertal was the home of Luftwaffe aircraft production and was heavily and repeatedly bombed during 1944/45.

Some days before this trip our crew's flight engineer, 'Wee Jock' Farquhar and I were sent to St Athens RAF near Cardiff in South Wales to be introduced to a new engine for the Halifax V1, one designated as the 600 series. St Athens was an RAF engineering unit and not an operational aerodrome.

Having checked in there the following day, we were in the workshops during the morning peering at the new engine and listening to an enthusiastic description from the manufacturer Bristol. At approximately 12.30pm we both went to the Officers Mess for a beer and some lunch.

We entered the Mess and were standing in the entrance hall discussing what we had seen when behind a service door, in the anteroom, there was a sound of some scuffling and the door opened and out stepped a Squadron Leader who came straight over to us, his hand held out to shake ours and said in a cheery voice, "I am Jack….." I never could recall his surname and he straight away said, "What do you know about predicted flak?" We said "Very little," we had never seen any instruction on the matter. He replied, "Well, I know all about it and this is what you need to know to avoid it."

He then proceeded to tell us in great detail about how a German radar guided predictive flak system worked. There was a German officer in charge of 5 or 6 guns, the most deadly Krup 88mm anti-aircraft guns. He explained that the radar equipment was used to ascertain the direction and altitude of an aircraft. He explained how long it took to extract a spent shell casing from the guns after having been fired, how long it took to reload the guns, how long it took to reset the angle and range of the salvo and finally how long it took for the shell to reach you at your detected altitude.

Out of all this, if you were missed by the first salvo, the next salvo would reach you in about 20 seconds and blow you out of the sky. He said that if you set a stop-clock and turned at 18 seconds to a new heading, 40 degrees to the left or right, you would not be hit. After further enquiries, he said he had to go, as he was in a hurry. He said goodbye, wished us good luck and left by the main door to the Mess.

I said to 'Wee Jock', "and what did you think of that?" to which he replied, "Makes you think, doesn't it." Typical of 'Wee Jock'! At that I looked at the door from which he had left and thought I'd just thank him more fully. Only a few seconds behind the hastily departing figure I bounded through the Mess doors.

Outside was a grass sward some 30 yards between the Mess and the nearest building. Despite being maybe 5 seconds behind him, when I looked left and right there was no-one in sight. Peculiar, maybe he ran but there was surely no necessity for that. Jock and I went into the bar and ordered up a couple of small beers. I said to the barman, "I've just met Squadron Leader Jack …." There were two barmen in attendance and both said together that there was no Officer on the station by that name. That came as a real surprise and on reflection I had noticed on the Squadron Leader's uniform that the top button on his tunic was undone. That signalled to me that he was at one time a Spitfire or Hurricane pilot during the Battle of Britain. But to be a Squadron Leader from Fighter Command, and to appear in an unusual way to give us a lecture on the subject of predictive flak, gave me the impression that he must have almost stood beside a German anti-aircraft gunnery emplacement with a stopwatch taking notes. And he was not a member of the St Athens unit? And was not known at that Station? Well, what do you think?

Well, his insistence that we listen and learn from his lecture was most earnest and left a deep impression on me.

The story has a sting in the tail. A couple of nights later we were detailed to bomb a target in Wuppertal. It was Friday 13th March 1945, not the best date for those who are superstitious. The raid consisted of 354 aircraft from 4, 6 and 8 Groups. 76 Squadron was assigned to be in the last wave over the target.

Wuppertal was still a tough target even in early 1945. Although the Luftwaffe was a defeated force, which now allowed the poorly armed RAF Halifax and Lancaster bombers to fly in daylight, Wuppertal was in the heart of the Ruhr valley and was home to an estimated 2 million German antiaircraft guns.

Over Northern France we were climbing up through a cold front to 18,000 feet. We flew into cloud at about 10,000ft and we found ourselves in a cell of unstable air which carried us up and then down wildly, accompanied by a wonderful display of St Elmo's fire. The aircraft was lit up with a dazzling display of static electricity playing around cockpit windows and the end of guns and propeller tips which were becoming glazed with ice. I kept the wings level known as 'flying altitude' but as we flew on through the cold-front in cloud the icing quickly built up on the leading edge of the wings and I saw the pitot-head tubes for the altimeter and airspeed begin to fall away. I decided to slowly descend the aircraft while maintaining altitude and we came out of cloud about 7,500ft. Now in the clear, the ice gradually disappeared, the speed came back and we started to regain height.

Back at 18,000ft and going in the last wave at the target the navigator reported that we would arrive there 20 minutes late. I decided to forget the planned target approach path and ordered a course correction to fly in a straight line to the target. In the event, we only saved about 6 minutes. The rest of the stream had gone and we were alone in clear air approaching the target. The Bomb Aimer, Charles, lined us up on residual fires glowing on the ground and we duly dropped our bombs on that point, there being too much cloud to make an accurate fix from 18,000ft. We proceeded to fly over one of the most heavily defended cities in the Ruhr alone.

Alerted, the anti-aircraft crews now turned their predicted flak on the only bomber in the sky.

"Bombs gone" came from Charles. As we headed for home the rear gunner reported "predicted flak starboard side, Skipper" and as I looked out I could see it in a long line of deadly grey-black puffs. With the words of our Squadron Leader from St Athens ringing in my mind, I immediately applied his 18 seconds rule and then turned quickly to starboard. Sure enough, another line of flack burst on our original track and after counting to 18 I turned and avoided it again, this time by altering course 40 degrees to the port. This went on for five more changes of heading as we dodged our way across the Wuppertal skies by which time the anti-aircraft flak batteries were out of range below and the flak stopped. I was later told that with the rear-gunner calling out the patterns of flak, nobody in the crew breathed for some minutes. Personally I can't remember breathing myself; just slowly counting to 18 and banking the aircraft hard at each random turn.

We proceeded on our way back to base without further incident.

Ever since that warning and insistent instruction in St Athens and its immediate success over Germany, I still ask myself, "Who was that Squadron Leader, where did he come from, where did he go and why unknown to other staff at St Athens?" Was it merely luck or good fortune meeting him? It makes you think, doesn't it.

Flying Officer Charles Gallagher

THE LAST ONE!

The morning of our final Operation broke clear and bright, today our last trip was a Daylight to a target, as I recall, somewhere in the Heligoland area of Germany in support of General Montgomery and the 1st British Army.

We stood third in the battle order for take-off. The first aircraft was airborne as we watched the second taking off – a young Crew on their first Operation of their Tour. The Skipper completely lost control of the sequence of throttling up his engines and as one engine after another lost then gained power, the aircraft began to swing violently from side to side as it picked up speed. Eventually, he lost control altogether, and as the aircraft swung one last time and the undercarriage finally gave way, the machine crashed down in the centre of the airfield at the intersection of the two main runways complete with seven crew, 15,000lbs of high explosives and a full-load of high-octane fuel, 2000 gallons. The crew were out of the down aircraft almost before it had come to a stop and then, together with all personnel in the immediate area, made for the nearest safe cover.

The stranded burning Halifax blew up some ten minutes later and the fact that the bombs were not armed until the aircraft was in flight gave the crew time to get away to safety. There was a massive explosion, the aircraft and a large section of the main runway had completely disappeared, in fact the Luftwaffe couldn't have done a better job. Many serious questions would have had to be asked and would have required very serious answers. Whatever happened to the unfortunate pilot of the aircraft we never heard but I'm sure it wasn't pleasant.

All aircraft, the remainder of the Squadron, were immediately ordered to their hard-standing dispersal points and eventually stood down from the Operation as the airfield was now out of action. Later that day our Crew learnt from our Flight Commander that we were Screened (Tour Completed) on our 29th Operation.

Of the party that night no memories are left, nor probably have they ever existed. We heard from others that it had been a great evening with all of us on top form.

THE TRIP WHEN CHARLES 'DIED'!

Mac writes.

21st May 1945. The war was now over in Europe and we were about to lose our Halifax as and when the iron-bomb dump was empty. This job meant daily trips out to sea and filling the North Sea with the Squadron's unused bombs in a 'safe' unarmed zone. This was a chore every member of the squadron was assigned to below the rank of Squadron Leader.

On one of these short missions, having dropped our load into the North Sea, we were returning to base at about 50ft over the sea all to cheer up the fishermen who responded with certain finger signs, and fist waving.

Suddenly there was a very loud 'bang' and the windscreen broke on impact of a bird strike with a herring gull. The gull landed with a thud on Charles's stomach and as he looked down with bird guts all over his anatomy, he let out a cry of "I'm dead Mac!". Looking at the mess around his torso, I commented on how lucky he was to be blessed with a feather lined stomach.

At that point reality set in and he seemed to return from the dead immediately. He retired to the rest area in the aircraft to clean up a bit and we returned to base with no further incidents.

What a cruel Skipper – we all laughed and I bought the beers that evening in the Mess.

Down the years I've often been asked;

"What made those days so special?"
There were many reasons but three tower above all others:
"Comradeship, the Crew and a Sense of Humour"
It was great to have known their friendship and a privilege to
have flown with them.
"Were it ever said there was never fear it could only be he was
never there."

INDIA

Late April 1945. Operational Tour completed, the Crew was sent on immediate Leave. Germany had been forced to accept unconditional surrender on the 8th May but we were still at war with Japan. After a week at home I went up to Scotland with Mac to his home near Dunoon, Argyllshire in Scotland, where almost immediately a telegram arrived; urgent recall to the Squadron. We reached Yorkshire and the Squadron the following morning and found it buzzing – When? Where? Type of aircraft? etc., etc. Secrecy surrounded us, the only answer was to where – Far East.

During the second half of May we dumped unwanted bombs into a disposal area in the North Sea.

My Log Book records that on June 7th we were airborne at 12.05 on our last flight in a Halifax, a low level trip over the Ruhr to show our Ground Crew the damage to the centre of Germany's manufacturing ability to make war. Large areas no longer existed, for example, Essen had been reduced to rubble.

Four days later on the 11th June we transferred from Bomber to Transport Command taking off on our first conversion flight to 2 engine Dakotas (DC3s).

Flying training started at once, sadly without our two Gunners, Jack Taylerson and Nic Nicholson and our Flight Engineer, Jock Farquhar, a huge personal loss to the rest of us but there was no job for them in the operation ahead.

Throughout July we continued converting to the Dakota, Formation and Low-level flying. Flying on the 11th August, with a huge mix of feelings, we left Yorkshire for the last time, three of the finest men I have known, and a year I will never forget.

Little did we know we would all be meeting again one day. This photograph shows the Crew reunited at the 76 Squadron Annual Reunion. Without Shep. Sadly, despite huge effort, we had been unable to find him from about three years after the war.

We arrived at Broadwell 2 hours later, an airfield near Whitney, Oxford, and current home of the 6th Airborne Division. We were to train and see action with them over Burma – the atmosphere was exciting and immediate. Training started two days later, Para trooping, towing Horsa gliders, supply dropping solo and in Formation.

Almost immediately the Americans dropped the first Nuclear Bomb on Hiroshima followed by a second on Nagasaki. Japan capitulated at once and it seemed our trip to India and the Far East would be cancelled. That night it became more of a Wake than a Party in the Mess, all the boyhood dreams were gone of India and the Far East.

Within 24 hours the plans had been changed again to bring back British ex-Japanese POWs across India to connect with long haul aircraft to fly them home. That night the Mess party 67 years ago will never be forgotten.

On the 29th August we left Broadwell for Portreath in Cornwall – "the First and the Last"- so named as it was the airfield of arrival from, or departure to, the Far East. For two weeks we relaxed in the fading heat of a beautiful summer, a more comfortable Mess than we had known before, beach parties, and the great sea food of the West Country, and in the only country in the world with the eternal excitement of never knowing what the weather would do – wonderful memories of long ago.

On the 16th of September the great day arrived. 76 Squadron was on the move to India, aircraft leaving at intervals throughout the day each carrying some 20 Ground Crew and Freight. My job had totally changed since our days as a Bomber Squadron now becoming officially a "Passenger and Freight officer," instantly renamed by the Crew "Panic and Fright" and greeted with delight and raucous approval by all. Our first night stop was Istres near Marseilles. There remains one memory, mosquitoes, hunter killers who met us and ate us on arrival. Thankfully it was one night only before we scratched and itched our way first to breakfast the following morning, and then across the Mediterranean passing

Sardinia, Malta and on to our second night stop at El Adem near Tobruk of 8th Army Desert Rat and Africa Corps fame on the North African coast. We arrived in El Adem after dark in 8½ hours flying, found good sleeping quarters, got to sleep, and were airborne for Lydda in Palestine at 06.15hrs the following morning. Should someone, and someone will, query the accuracy of times, dates, and places I have my Log Book and a huge file of letters home carefully kept at home throughout the war in front of me as I write – times are accurate to the minute! After 4 hours flying we reached Lydda, fixed as always the accommodation for our Ground Crew, and went to an open air cinema on the camp in the evening. The following day we had free time until 22:00hrs before leaving Lydda and decided on a visit to Jerusalem as our top priority. An early start in the morning, got hold of a truck, and after 1½ hours through rocky sandy passes covered in olive trees we arrived.

Looking back over the 3 days since we left Cornwall it now seemed that we were making good the lazy inactivity on its beautiful beaches and wonderful coast.

We had an excellent lunch in the Officer's club in Jerusalem and then left on an organized guided tour of the City. A quote from my letter home on 21st September "we first went up to the Mount of Olives by car and saw the little Church of the Ascension, a magnificent view of the City and its walls and the Hill of Calvary and the Dead Sea with its deep blue looking superb against sand and mountains on all sides.

It was a perfect day, warm and sunny. After this we motored to Bethlehem and I enjoyed this part best of all – the Church of the Nativity – it is beautiful inside and fascinating. Down in the vaults below what is supposed to be the actual Manger where Christ was born though I imagine a great deal of doubt and controversy exists, and finally the Christmas Bells broadcast every Christmas. I forgot to say that before Bethlehem we went into the Garden of Gethsemane, most beautifully kept, and the lovely little Church. I think the Franciscan monks look after it." Much food for thought and discussion on the drive back to Lydda.

At 22:00hrs we left Lydda for Wadihalfa and Khartoum but lost our starboard engine over Port Said requiring immediate diversion to an American airfield in the Cairo area. The Ground Crew stayed on camp to repair the engine and the Crew had a couple of hours sleep in Cairo before being recalled as the engine was now serviceable. We took off again at midday for Khartoum. About an hour later the engine failed again so we diverted at once to RAF Almaza. The Ground Crew again stayed on camp to make repairs while the four of us; Mac, Jim, Shep and I were driven to the Helio Palace Hotel in Cairo.

During the next 7 days we returned to air test the aircraft several times, the Skipper snagging it each time. Finally we returned to find the engine ok after air test and were airborne on a 4 hour flight to Wadihalfa. By sheer chance of engine failure the four of us had seven days in what to us was a luxury hotel, a trip to the pyramids, a couple of rides on a camel and an interesting view of Cairo night life while the Ground Crew ground it out repairing the aircraft – Great Guys – they took it well as they always did.

On landing at Wadihalfa and opening the aircraft door we were hit in the face by a biting hot wind and even hotter sand. I have no idea what the place is like today, only the memory of a most unattractive bit of desert 67 years ago.

We took an hour off for a well-earned breakfast and thankfully left for Khartoum arriving there 3 hours later. We found a fine peace time RAF station but very hot and humid. The following day after leaving at 07:03hrs we reached Aden after 6 hours in the air and enjoying the wonderful mountain scenery in Eritrea.

Leaving Aden for Karachi at 03:00hrs the following morning we landed 7½ hours later at Masira, a small island off the south coast of Arabia, got some sleep, and then on to Karachi landing with one thought in mind – sleep!

We found we would be under canvas at first, two to a tent, stone floor and cupboard which all seemed cooler than billets. In fact we hopped over to Mauripa next day, another Karachi airfield followed by 8 enjoyable days there. We then received an urgent order to take water to Jiwani some 2½ hours flying along the coast of Baluchistan – they were running short! There being no runway we landed on a dirt track!

In 1986, 40 years later, my daughter Kate and I, were returning from Delhi in a BOAC Tri-Star after a wonderful 3 week holiday in India and Kashmir. The Captain asked us up to the flight deck and I told him the story of our trip to Jiwani all those years ago. I think he enjoyed it.

During October we made three trooping flights between Poona and Karachi and one down to Madras. Sadly the trip to Madras was the end of my flying days as all who had come out from the UK as passenger and freight officers were to be replaced by pilots to fly as second pilots while we were posted to Karachi to establish a ground passenger and freight operation, "108 Wing Operations" similar to Traffic in a Civil Airline. Obviously leaving the last of the Crew, Mac, Jim and Shep was the saddest part of it although

Shep was due to be demobbed shortly and Mac within the next 6 months or so but losing Poona for Karachi was a major loss also. We had a great time during our 2 months based in Poona, 2,000 feet up cool at night, beautiful green mountains all around us, excellent cricket and squash, a wonderful Mess and super food – a poor exchange for the Sindh Desert!

Amongst many other things at this time the Governor of Bombay invited guests from the various Service Messes in the region to a House Party at Government House to hear a Welsh choir which was on tour, superb event. Luckily half a dozen of us had been invited from Poona and it seemed that most of the Indian princes and their maharanis were there too dripping with jewellery worth millions as they stood – a seriously magnificent sight.

On the 17th November a cable arrived from Dad telling me of the award of the DFC announced in the London Gazette of the 6th of November and in the local Papers together with the Citation. Mac, Jim and I had all received the award of the Distinguished Flying Cross.

To me this was above all a Crew Award as the seven of us had depended completely on each other – total Trust, total Comradeship and a Sense of Humour.

At this point those of us who had finished flying left for Karachi and found ourselves in the Killarney Hotel where we were to live – a nice enough place. We discovered a Museum was to be our work base which seemed a rather sad but entirely appropriate name for it, such was our mood at that time, but we would get over it!

We did in fact get into the swing of things quickly, my job as assistant controller in the Operations Room was a little more interesting than I had imagined. However, with the war over the work load was relatively light to anything we had known before which gave us a lot of time for Sport. Early December to late January was cool and then heated up quickly, cricket, squash, and tennis were all playable from around 5pm in the evening, the ground being too hard for rugby. I believe it was late February when a new person came into my life. The new person was a monkey about 4ft high. I was asked if I would like to have him. In a silent moment of shock and insanity I agreed while completely ignorant of his preferred lifestyle, his food, and the accommodation he would like in someone else's hotel. I called him Jimmy.

The female Polish manageress of the hotel knew nothing of all this. The first couple of days were surprisingly uneventful except for his apparent determination to show us that he could swim in the little pond in the garden and enjoyed doing it, a kind of breast stroke. He had survived his night accommodation in a reasonably adequate garden shed. However a dramatic change about the sixth day when he went to war with a fat middle aged Army Major on liaison to our Mess whose habit was to enjoy a large cigar in the shade of a tree after lunch. Jimmy noticed this as he appeared to notice everything and climbed onto a branch immediately above the Major's head. Out came the cigar, in a flash Jimmy had it in his hands and sat slowly shredding it – I saw it all! It was quite amazing how quickly and neatly it was done.

It was our habit in hot weather, now continuous, to lie out in the shade on our excellent bedroom balconies. Suddenly there was a dreadful moaning scream to a background of breaking glass. Several of us rushed to the room of the manageress and there she sat at her dressing table with Jimmy sitting on top of it smashing her scent bottles together. Jimmy left that night! I had no worry about his future. He loved life, got on well with people, and was a natural entrepreneur. He would succeed. I paid for damages. Our Polish lady was a good sport and all was forgiven.

In early March the Indian navy mutinied in Karachi and Bombay. The only direct effect it had on us was that for around a fortnight we had to carry side arms while in the town of Karachi. The Ghurkhas took control of the cruiser lying in Karachi harbour by direct assault while just prior to this the cruiser had fired into our tennis courts or that is where two shells fortunately did not explode. Spitfires flew low over Bombay and the mutiny finished after about a week.

Sitting in the Mess one day I answered the telephone and who should be on the other end of the line but Shep our Wireless Operator. It turned out that Shep was on his way home on demob leave. You will recall that at 27 he was incredibly old and on an earlier release to the rest of the Crew. We both spoke together – "where shall we meet?" and bearing in mind he had to leave the following morning by air to the UK we still had a magnificent dinner.

At this time during the Indian Naval Mutiny in Karachi four of us were billeted for a short while in a bungalow in the Town. 2 of us slept in side rooms and a young officer who had recently joined us shared the entrance hall with me.

One evening we were all sitting in a bar in town, three of us decided on an early night while the newcomer said that he would join us later at the bungalow.

Nothing strange in this but we had noticed that for a short while he had seemed increasingly highly strung drinking too much and apparently obsessed by the distinguished career of his elder brother, while he himself had not been operational in the RAF. This was simply due to his being unable to finish his training and join a squadron before the end of the war.

It must have been around midnight, the three of us were back in bed and I would guess probably half asleep. The front door opened and he walked in. He didn't turn the light on but sat down at the centre table, lit a candle some ten paces from my bed.

Pulling out his service revolver he pointed it directly at me holding it steady and level for what must have been about a minute and felt like 50 – the range point blank.

I was now fully awake! He then walked to his kit bag on the other side of the room and came back with a different hand gun and followed exactly the same procedure twice more – the last time with a small gun which I found later belonged to a woman.

In a large dark room lit by just one candle with a revolver levelled at you at point blank range at near midnight creates a difficult background to making serious decisions – I had decided to appear asleep, there would be less to do.

On returning to the table he put the little revolver down and once again picked up his Service revolver, turned round, strode to the bathroom, closed the door behind him. There were two shots, the saddest form of death.

The three of us were with him in seconds; there was nothing we could do. How desperately sad we had not recognised the weight of pressures that had proved too much.

Our RAF Karachi Headquarters had the local CID around within a matter of minutes and two of their men sat on the end of my bed for I believe a couple of hours questioning us.

The following morning an RAF Pathologist questioned us again and confirmed suicide.

My memory, although acutely aware of what happened that night, may be marginally inaccurate concerning the details of consequent events – broadly they were as follows. I was put in charge of his personal effects; extraordinary discoveries were now made regarding his life which had led to his problems. A number of papers and letters relating to suicide, murder and assassinations were found, some describing how he believed he would become personally involved in this way of life. It seemed like reading fiction but we came to realize that the 3 of us might well have been fortunate that night.

The funeral was a serious problem. Being a Roman Catholic

his Priests were unable to bury him, but the matter was eventually resolved.

Some few years later I was travelling from Victoria to Purley when I picked up an evening paper and saw by sheer chance "distinguished officer shoots himself in London flat". It was his brother.

LATE APRIL 1946

"Eric Day, I can't believe it!" That was how two 22 year olds met again in a RAF Mess in India 4 years after joining the University Air Squadron at Cambridge in April 1942. I doubt the beers' arrival took longer than a minute, the second perhaps a little faster. Questions flew thick and fast. Answers unable to keep pace – Friendships, Humour, Training, Squadron life, Operations, Girlfriends – exaggeration overwhelming fact, just life in the RAF.

We had much in common after Cambridge, Eric posted to Canada for flying training while I did mine in South Africa both returning to the UK a year later, Eric a Pilot while I came back a Navigator/Bomb Aimer. After Operational Training in the UK we were posted to Bomber Command Squadrons on Lancasters and Halifaxes.

Both of us were fortunate.

Questions and answers for the time exhausted the subject turned to Leave – the war over it now seemed possible. That evening seated in front of the Adjutant, two young men, a generation of boys reared on tales of the old India, Kipling and the North West Frontier, and for mental stimulation the Hotspur, Wizard and the Boys Own Paper were presenting their case for 3 weeks leave, the war being over and won, in no small part due to their personal entry into it!

Hitchhiking an aircraft the following morning from Karachi to Delhi we arrived in time to catch the Frontier Mail to Rawalpindi, a journey never to be forgotten but not to be fully enjoyed as two Indians sharing our carriage spread a superb curry that we could only watch and admire.

All this to a very English background conversation recording that great summer at Cambridge – parties, punting up the Granta with a gramophone, a girl or perhaps more, to the Green Man at Granchester and a pint or perhaps three, a four wheel bicycle, one of only two in England, the last man having to jump on the rear seat while moving and the night Trinity Hall College next door to us at Sidney Sussex was machine gunned by a lone Heinkel bomber during our farewell party at the end of our Course. How might we have come to know each other's ways had we known something of each other's language?

Following a sleepless night and a request for a major breakfast the sun rose over a little terrace in the North West Inn at Rawalpindi. A breakfast that would ensure the health of an RAF Squadron was secured followed by two seats in a little bus starting early for Srinagar, the capital of Kashmir. We joined the Jhelum Valley, the ancient passage for the river and the little road that had for centuries borne travellers to Kashmir and the North. The wild and rocky river brought memories of the lonely beauty of Dartmoor, my boyhood home. Seemingly rope bridges offered occasional uninviting crossings.

At the first sight of the Himalayan Foothills and the snow peaks beyond we could only ask the driver to stop the bus and watch in wonder.

On arriving in Srinagar late in the evening rooms were booked at the Regina Hotel which was ideally situated to meet the challenge of exploring the mighty Dal Lake. Shikaras, little open boats roofed and curtained against the sun, provided the perfect way. In the next two days we visited several little islands where it was fascinating to watch a variety of things being made, jewellery, carpets, woollen shawls, woodwork, the wonderful crafts of Kashmir.

Each morning shikaras filled with market flowers formed little floral pageants and inspired thoughts from far-away of the haunting line from Coleridge "as idle as a painted ship upon a painted ocean." We walked the gardens of Nishath and Shalimar and marvelled at the Moghul summer houses built by their Emperors 400 years ago when they turned their elephants north to escape the heat of a Delhi summer.

We left early on the third day for Gulmarg in a little bus so full of Locals that surely few could survive the 25 miles we had to go. However we found the final 4 were on mountain ponies – I believe we owed our lives to them.

It was a kind of Kashmiri triathlon – the bus, the ponies and the almost vertical climb over the last few miles. The very old were carried up in baskets attached to long poles. We made it!

8000 ft. up in the Himalayan foothills a pine hut in the village of Gulmarg, so beautifully in English – The Meadow of Flowers – became our final home in Kashmir. The memory here needs no base of letters – it is forever.

Two little Kashmiri ponies, their sure feet and mountain wisdom, carried us daily through the wonders of the springtime wilderness of rock and pine forest, sometimes along sheer ledges curiously described as mountain paths. The ever climbing snow line drawn higher by the springtime sun invited flowers to wake from sleep and look toward the sky.

The ponies watched our picnic lunches patient and still. How priceless their thoughts could we know they may have had. Grey mist would sometimes roll a silent cloak across the day. On others sunlit snow peaks would rise in glory to the north. Surely there could be few places of wild and remote beauty on this earth where mystery and fantasy could suggest to two young travellers that possibly, just possibly no one else had ever seen.

A wonderful holiday and memories forever for us both.

On our return to Karachi we found our Mess had been moved to the 2nd Indian Airborne camp just outside Karachi, a Mess with some 50 ex aircrew officers.

Strange looking back that we had come so close to seeing action with the 6th British Airborne Division only to be stopped by Japan's capitulation and now to camp with the 2nd Indian Airborne during our final months in the Service.

Our work had not changed but socially it changed to meet the heat of a Karachi summer and our new neighbours. Cricket sprang to life – I raised a cricket team, and we called it Karachi Area Control. We played two or sometimes three matches a week against Service sides and became quite a useful team. Games started after

5pm which enabled us to fit in the work as well! Cricket, tennis, squash, boating – all had excellent clubs and life had become great fun, and looked promising for the rest of the year when we were due to be "demobbed". We spent most weekends at Hawkes Bay, a lovely little beach close to Karachi. Great picnics, BBQs were the order of the day.

As the weather got hotter it was fascinating to watch baby turtles cracking their eggs as they left their sand dune incubation and scuttled down to the sea, regrettably, often straight into the mouths of large fish cruising in the shallows.

The Senior Officer in the Mess was a Wing Commander Jock Hunter, a large Scot of around 6ft 4ins tall and a character. He was one of a few survivors of the Fairy Battle light bomber squadrons who attacked the bridges over the rivers of Northern France in an attempt to halt the German breakthrough in 1940 – most were shot down.

Many of us were in demob release group 49 and due to leave India in late October. We heard that the Winco (Wing Commander) was planning a farewell Party and that he felt that it should be an "event" as he put it. Knowing Jock pretty well we had no doubt that it would be – it was.

We left Karachi on the following morning, the 10th October 1946 arriving in Worli, a suburb of Bombay, that day.

The weather was already cooler in Karachi and starting to get pleasant in Bombay. We had a great 3 weeks waiting for a ship to take us home. As I have no record of the farewell party itself written during the following fortnight I won't attempt detail 68 years later. Only that it was judged by the airborne boys as being remarkable! I do have details of our final 3 weeks. We spent much of our time in the open air swimming pool with an admirable bar/café alongside it at Breach Candy, another suburb of Bombay facing the sea.

While sightseeing we came across one of India's Cricket Test grounds. A glorious green square and outfield unlike the matting we had to play on at Karachi. Finally in mid-November we sailed for home in the SS Lancashire, the last of the purpose built troop ships.

As we crossed the Indian Ocean on those warm far away evenings we sat out on deck at the stern of the ship talking of the lives we had known and of all that the future might hold.

A school of whales joined us as if wanting to escort us across their sea and perhaps say farewell as we left it – who knows what these great creatures thought. We then sailed home via the Suez Canal bringing back memories of 3 years earlier coming home from South Africa and finally docked once again at Liverpool.

Thoughts raced amongst the years as it seemed I watched the disembarkation of a generation who had forged a life at 18 and lived one before they grew old.

1229 R. Hoffmann,
Southampton.　　　H.M.T. "LANCASHIRE."　　9,543 TONS.
Length 502 Feet.　　Breadth 57 Feet.

CIVVY STREET

While still in India I was asked with several others whether I would volunteer to serve in the Occupation Force in Japan for one year before demobilization – undoubtedly interesting, possibly exciting but short term. As I had now to be thinking way into the future I turned it down.

Looking back to my entry into the RAF via the university Air Squadron at Cambridge in the summer of 1942 I recall how the 50 of us on the Course were told that if we applied to continue the academic side that we had done in the six months we were there it would count as the first year of a degree. It was a good and generous offer but the more I thought about it at the time I could not see myself getting my head around a desk again after the previous five years – I decided no.

However the connection between my old school Blundells, Cambridge University and the Royal Air Force was interesting. I asked Amber Oliver, the Blundells Development Director, if she could tell me anything of particular interest about those days. Kindly she wrote as follows:

'Blundells association with the Sidney Sussex College, Cambridge, began in 1603 with the establishment of two Scholarships and two Fellowships at the College, to be filled by boys from the school. This arrangement remained in force until 1860 when as a result of an overhaul of the University's awards Blundells share was restricted to three scholarships. Such closed scholarships continued to be available to Blundells students until 1978 in which year the final Sidney Sussex exhibition was awarded. There are currently plans in progress to explore the viability of re-establishing the provision for these awards. In addition there were on occasions minor scholarships awarded to Blundells pupils rather than the main exhibition awards. For a short degree – Cambridge University awarded a degree on the basis of five terms academic work plus a period of National Service. The number of terms did vary during the war.'

Dare I suggest that an old clothier from Tiverton in Devon, Peter Blundell, may smile down occasionally on the school he created those long years ago and has seen develop from the good school I knew so well to the great one I saw on a visit last year – perhaps even enjoy a chuckle to an imaginary friendship with the Royal Air Force at a momentous period in our country's history.

1947

On my return home from India it was great to find Mum, Dad, my sister Norah and Sarie in their new home, the little village of Owermoigne just seven miles east of Dorchester. Dorset had always been their final goal.

Sarie gave me a wild welcome. She was, as you may remember, my border collie puppy who 'joined' our Crew during training at Stanton Harcourt and then had to be quickly removed to my home on Dartmoor after she disgraced herself by chewing up most of our socks and pants in the Nissan hut where we slept.

My objective now was to get a job interview and to my delight a positive reply came back from British South American Airways (BSAA). This new airline had been formed with Air Vice Marshal Don Bennett as Chief Executive. He had commanded the Pathfinder Force of Bomber Command and was one of the outstanding airmen of the Second World War.

I was hopeful that this would mean ex Bomber Command personnel would have an edge in selection! Detail of my interview has long gone but I do recall that I liked the man who interviewed me and all that he told me about the business. I can only assume that he saw a glimmer of hope as he looked across the desk as I got a job offer in Traffic (passenger and freight). You may recall that in India I had a similar job in the RAF renamed instantly by the Crew as 'Panic and Fright'.

Within four weeks I found myself amongst a sprawl of huts at London Airport actually working in a hut not dissimilar to the ones we had slept in throughout RAF days.

It is strange to think of the city of computers and technology that stands today and the relative cluster of huts that we worked in through the bitterly cold winter of 1947. As expected ex-Bomber Command people formed many of the personnel I worked with and virtually all of the Aircrews.

In late February I got a phone call from the senior Traffic Officer asking me to come along for a chat – now. The emphasis on the final word was worrying and my mind raced from instant dismissal to a slower form of the same thing.

I left his office in unconcealed excitement – I was to go for around three months on a temporary posting to relieve someone who had to return to the UK for a while.

Before he finished talking I had assured him that as the most junior person in BSAA I would do any possible task should he wish to extend the assignment!

From a letter home I see that I arrived in Bermuda on the 20th March 1948. We flew out in a 13 seat Lancastrian, the civil version of the Lancaster Bomber. As there were thirteen delightful elderly ladies plus two air hostesses I realized my comfort would be subject to general consent! I quickly discovered each was a millionairess owning her own Company and went regularly on holiday together – their leader – for instance owning Dixons Greeting Cards. A pleasant night's stop-over in Lisbon.

The following day we crossed to the Azores where I was delighted to meet up with John Blowes again not seen since early days at London Airport.

No concern at leaving the Azores which in a letter home I described as a lonely and desolate place.

The long trip to Bermuda from the Azores will live forever in my memory. Four of those intrepid ladies decided they would teach me to play bridge. My reaction in two words was terror and escape. I had never been so terrified in an aeroplane before. All I had ever played in earlier times was called Troop Ship Solo, a very rustic form of cards. Mercifully they played while I watched and grunted as intelligently as I could.

I see we landed in Bermuda at 2 am local time so probably got to sleep around 3 am. I was billeted at the White Horse Tavern on St. George's Island where the legendary Arthur Woodman and his wife hosted the BSAA staff and the Aircrews who night stopped in Bermuda before flying the next aircraft down the West Coast of South America to Santiago. I had three fabulous months living in this wonderful and genuinely unique place.

At 8am the following morning I walked into the BSAA office, not too bad timing! The first thing I was given was a note from the leader of our ladies' group asking if I would care to join them at 6pm at the Bermudiana Hotel in Hamilton. They had arranged a little jaunt around the island that evening.

The first day was spent acclimatizing to the office and its procedures and a quick dash to the shops to acquire a light weight suit for the evening, and it would be needed anyway. – remember I had to try and keep pace with odds of 13:1 against. I refer to the 13 ladies.

In those days transport consisted of one little single Track railway, scores of small pony drawn carriages and around 500 cars. Before the war only the Governor had a car. The ponies and their carriages were a delight. Imagine at night with their lanterns swinging as they trotted around the island, little specks of light dancing in the dark. It was magical. Spread across the island little Bars popped up pretty and welcoming, it was an evening in a life time and in the occasional lucid moment at the time I recall thinking what a splendid rugby team the ladies would have made only a year or two earlier, both on and most certainly off the field!

I recall saying "Goodbye" around 4am-ish but nothing is very certain other than they were a very interesting, much travelled and delightful group of people.

In '48 and '49 we sadly lost two of our Tudor aircraft, Star Tiger and Star Ariel, with all Passengers and Crew – I knew both Crews well. Star Tiger disappeared on the 29th January 1948 without trace on the long leg from Santa Maria in the Azores to Bermuda – some 13 hours flying. Star Ariel left Bermuda for Kingston Jamaica on the 17th January 1949 in perfect weather and was never heard of again – a complete mystery. Both crews were highly experienced ex-Bomber Command and had considerable experience also of BSAA.

How do I describe this wonderful island from cycling all over it and many carriage rides. My memory has no doubt – the glory of colour in a Bermuda spring.

The deep blue of the sea against a background of sand, cedar woodland and fields of arum lilies – a huge market flown daily to New York. Oleanders in their simple splendour, the white and pink of almost every building on the island, the ponies and their little carriages, coves, inlets and tiny islands – all create this pageant of the sea.

I realized early on that I would miss the White Horse as much as anything when it came to leave this magical island for it was very much part of the magic. The White Horse stood along one side of St. George's Square. From the veranda looking across the square we were faced by a Breakfast Club that actually served anything at any time, and to your right the tiny harbour little more than a wharf and seriously picturesque.

Arthur and his wife, her name I have sadly forgotten, were the masters of informality and had created a superb atmosphere akin I suspect more to the 19th than the 20th century as the way of life at "Arthur's" yet having the same level of efficiency and modern facilities of a good hotel.

After 65 years I have a vivid memory of the most enjoyable kitchen I have known where two large local lady cooks produced and served the most enormous meals to the air crew and staff (average age 25 years) at any hour of the day or night and always with a laugh or a smile under any pressure – what a priceless personal gift! They were simply fantastic and had a massive effect on morale and my memory!

The Company allowed me to take my 2 weeks annual leave while out there so towards the end of June I set off to share it between Jamaica, Nassau and Bermuda.

The arrival at Kingston Jamaica was extraordinary, there was no noticeable sign of life at the airport; nothing appeared to actually move. An elderly woman who had presumably noticed I was looking for something grunted along the lines "You want something?" Alas a lost cause was staring me in the face. "It's the cricket, you see, they are all watching or listening. And the score is not good, you see. And it's Barbados, you see."

By this time I had no illusions and my vision was perfect. The question remained when was the final day of the match for my holiday would depend on it as until then Jamaica was dead.

As far as memory will take me it was the last day and I had four wonderful days including a trip to the Blue Mountains with their ceiling of around 8,000ft necessitated a good sweater after the heat of the beaches.

Nassau was just a couple of night stops with as much exploring as possible in the time, then back to life in Bermuda. In the final few days we had some wonderful Beach parties followed by superb supper parties. Looking back on the three to four months in Bermuda we certainly had a marvellous time out there, worked hard and learnt a great deal.

Having arrived back in England I was told immediately of my posting to Dakar in French West Africa and had a couple of days down in Dorset to see the family.

A search to find letters home or a diary written while out there has revealed nothing. However, three events during that time will never be forgotten.

A member of staff met me at Yoff airport on arrival from London and Lisbon and as we shook hands told me that I would need a mosquito net at night. I felt it strange that this should be the priority message on arrival perhaps a warning of something else to come. That was nothing to what followed. "It's best to wear nothing at night as they get under the net and chew everything they see." Confidence was now in free fall. My posting was for 12 months – at this moment to survive one appeared unlikely. Dog tired I got to sleep early and woke up in a pool of sweat and cockroaches everywhere chewing pieces of newspaper all over me – no exaggeration. For a while I fought a battle with the cockroaches. I won. I had to win. It would have been serious indeed had I not.

I recall one evening meeting a crowd of English men in one of the Dakar bars who turned out to be the Crew of the Zini a merchantman of the Holt line on a short visit to Dakar. The five of us were off duty and they asked us to join them on the ship for a can or two of beer. The following morning I remember Daboo, one of our young drivers, trying to understand why the back of our little open Austen car had changed its shape from convex to concave – it had been parked almost touching the Zini which in turn lay almost touching the key side. Sixty three years later I have no idea how it came about!

Daboo & Self (left) The Car (right)

The last memorable event I can remember was our final visit to an all night club mostly out of doors. The Jardin d'Ete, very French. On these visits we had come to know some of the French members quite well and we agreed it would be appropriate to make a little gesture of friendship one evening at the club. The 21st of October being Trafalgar Day was selected and our plans were carefully rehearsed for we knew it could go horribly wrong.

One who shall be nameless would step on to our table waving happily at everyone. Huge black moustache and superbly equipped for the part he would burst into "Rule Britannia". We would all join in and then stand and hold our breath – there was a roar of applause that confirmed that we had got it right – we could have been skinned alive!

Inspired and now conducted by a wildly excited Frenchman we sang, hummed and stumbled our way through the Marseillaise accompanied by a roar from the French. I thought the sky would descend – we were buddies!

After the years' duty ended I returned to the UK happy that we had worked pretty hard, had fun, gained a lot of experience – but Dakar was not Bermuda. It's so long ago to look back now, over 65 years. I remember a young company that had in its quality of people the ability to take it far.

It was sad to know that shortly we would be absorbed by another company.

I joined the sales force of Thomas Hedley on the 1st January 1952. The company was in fact owned by Procter and Gamble of the United States but it didn't take the name of P & G until 1962 in the UK. A great deal has changed in the last half century with the dominant share of the business having moved from the independent to the multiple sector. Also much has naturally had to alter structurally in the Sales Force to meet this change. If asked why I spent 35 years with P & G it largely speaks for itself, where it does not there are factors that mattered a great deal to me. Work could be hard provided it was interesting and enjoyable and family life could be lived to the full. It was if you were in P & G – the balance was right.

I had a number of great friends over the years in P & G, some sadly now missing, including two great personal friends Ken Rodhouse and Alan Vallis.

I remember a great Company and the pride in being part of it with its foremost qualities of Training, Leadership and Motivation.

In September 1986 three of us, Ken, Alan and I, all Area Managers, were given a Retirement Party at Goodwood House, West Sussex.

A beautiful Park and House, we had a guided tour before sitting down to an excellent dinner. Each of us gave a talk afterwards about our life in the Company. May I tell you a little story that I told amongst other things that evening.

The Company payment procedure allowed a discount on prompt payment on our goods. It was around my third month in the Company, I was a new boy, probably on my third day or so on my own without my trainer and having finished my initial training as a salesman. After preparing the days' work on the evening before, I had noticed that one large account had lost his discount through being late on payment and would have to be handled particularly carefully.

When I entered the store with an air of cheerful confidence which in no way did I feel, and knowing his discount problem, as expected he made no fraternal rush to greet me! When he finally got closer I could see he was a most unhappy grocer. Looking down at my paper work, for somehow I had to feel busy at something, it struck me across the face; it was wet, soft and smelt of fish. I recognized, lying on the floor, one of the salmon I had seen when coming into the shop and seem to remember wondering if this could be the only career I would eventually enjoy – it all seemed rather dramatic and perhaps a bit over the top. The assistant standing by told me later that it was a brilliantly executed shot by his boss. Shortly afterwards, to my amazement, there was my grocer holding the required cash in one hand while trying to shake mine with the other. I found later that he liked my reaction – apparently I had smiled!

I little imagined starting out that day that my top priority as a civilian would become survival! It must be said that that was the only call I ever made in 35 years of that nature.

THE MEMORIAL
BOMBER COMMAND
GREEN PARK LONDON

JUNE 2012

For 67 years Bomber Command and the 55,573 men who never came back would wait to be honoured and remembered by the nation.

On the 28th June 2012 Her Majesty the Queen unveiled a memorial so stunning for its inspired vision and beauty that it now stands amongst the great sculptures of the world, depicting a group of a 7 man Bomber Crew in bronze created by the brilliant sculptor Philip Jackson, ensuring these men will remain with us forever.

For the work of the volunteers who dedicated a part of their lives to the memorial it is simply a triumph.

The ceiling is made from the aluminium of a Halifax bomber shot down over Belgium in 1944. Due to the height and scale of the sculptures they can always be seen against a background of sky both day and night.

On the evening of the 27th June to our amazement, delight and without warning Rosanne, one of my daughters, walked through the front door having just flown in from Spain.

On the following morning my wife Mary, Rosanne and I met my grandson, Richard, at Victoria Station around 9.15am.

The four of us got a free taxi to Green Park, site of the Memorial. A decision not to charge Veterans having been taken by London Black Cab taxis on this occasion, so typical a gesture of many others on that wonderful day. Mary and I had tickets for the Memorial area of some 500 seats where Mac and his son James would join us. Richard, with his ticket to the Salute area of some 7000 seats would join Simon, my nephew. Rosanne, having only been able to come at the last minute had just a hope of getting one – it paid off and she joined Richard and Simon in the Salute area – fair justice after a marvellous effort to come. By now the weather had changed from cloudy warm to sky blue hot. Green Park looked gorgeous – London was just showing off.

On arriving at Green Park we were greeted by a mix of Regulars and University Air Squadron Cadets with a level of courtesy and helpfulness I can only describe as unsurpassable. It created a wonderful atmosphere throughout the day.

Mary and I were shown into the first of the refreshment marquees and as I recall some twenty Aussies in their slouch hats were coming in at the same time at an average age I would guess of 88 – 92. They made no attempt to stay in an Aussie "huddle" but spread themselves immediately around the various tables.

A 92 year old Rear Gunner sat down next to Mary and immediately, in a delightful way, started to tell her of his thoughts on arrival in England in 1943 and mighty interesting some of them were! Many a great chat before moving on to the memorial area with Mac and James who had just joined us for the Service of Dedication and the arrival of Her Majesty the Queen.

MY MEMORIES AND THOUGHTS

Magnificent and moving
Memories of people and days long gone
Pride in the men and women who served and serve today in
the Royal Air Force

In a changing world the Message stands:

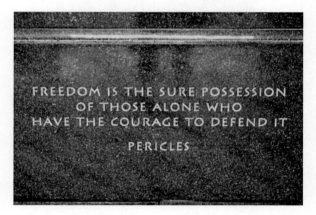

FREEDOM IS THE SURE POSSESSION
OF THOSE ALONE WHO
HAVE THE COURAGE TO DEFEND IT

PERICLES

Philip Jackson

On July 26th, almost exactly a month after the Memorial Service, my eldest daughter Caroline knowing how much Mary and I would love to meet Philip Jackson had arranged for us to see him at his studio and gallery. We needed to be there not later than 2pm as he was giving a talk to an art group at 2.30pm. We could then have a good chat first. Most kindly and generously he also asked us to join the group at the talk and for a delicious tea afterwards. What can I say of the afternoon that the three of us spent at that beautiful gallery near Midhurst? To have the privilege and delight of meeting this extraordinary and great man and to hear his Talk was a memorable culmination to a major month of my life.

The Studio

A strange feeling as we entered with the towering figures of a Bomber Crew looking down.

(Self, Mary, Philip Jackson in his workshop. Photo taken by my daughter Caroline)

76 SQUADRON (R)
LINTON – ON – OUSE
YORKSHIRE

September 2012. At the kind invitation of the Squadron some of the few remaining members of the old 76 Halifax Squadron were their guests for the weekend of the 21st – 23rd September 2012.

Mac's son James drove Mary, Mac and me up to Yorkshire where we met my daughter Kate, son-in-law Joe and granddaughter Rosie who joined us for the weekend at Linton.

We had a great welcome and a superb weekend masterminded by F/Lt Martin Wintermeyer with the help of F/Lt Nick Graham.

A great first evening was spent in the Mess Bar and during the evening Mac and I were each unexpectedly presented with a fine picture of Tucanos by the Station Commander Group Captain David Cooper – all signed by their Crews and with the call-sign "Q" Queenie, the old call-sign of our Halifax 68 years ago – a hugely appreciated gesture.

The following morning, after breakfast, we visited the Memorial Room. A fascinating talk on the history of the various Squadrons and particular events at Linton during the war followed, given by the curator.

Afterwards, while looking at various memorabilia around the room, Mary found at long last a history of her two cousins – Tony and Hugh O'Neil – who had both distinguished themselves as Fighter Pilots. Tony, the elder served in Bomber Command from the first day of the war and was shot down over Belgium, then managing to get home safely. Towards the end of the Battle of Britain he transferred to Fighter Command and later commanded a Fighter Squadron in India. Hugh served in Fighter Command throughout. Tony was awarded the DFC; Hugh the DFC and Bar.

The curator very kindly made immediate contact with Tony's daughter who agreed we should meet shortly for lunch – how strange the twists and turns of life.

Immediately after lunch, we left for Elvington – the Halifax museum – some 3 miles outside York. "Friday the 13th" is the only complete Halifax left in Britain though in Canada I believe two more exist – none anywhere being airworthy.

How incredible – 68 years ago – had I known that I would be clambering around this one with daughter Kate and granddaughter Rosie – hugely enjoyed by all three of us, and my wife Mary looking on.

Glorious weather and wonderful memories.

Back to the Squadron at Linton in time for dinner in the Mess, an excellent dinner hosted by Martin and a moving and memorable speech from George French, Chairman of the old 76 Halifax Squadron Association.

As many will know, the Gods had smiled on George on one occasion when he and his crew were preparing to land on return from a night operation – when an enemy night fighter intruder shot their aircraft down and he had to bail out at 400ft. – an unfriendly height to leave your aircraft by parachute. Interesting thoughts at the dinner table suggested that so close is the Linton circuit to that of our old Holme-on-Spalding airfield that George might have landed that night – with a slight touch of imagination – on the exact spot occupied by the table in front of him!

The following morning, over to Holme-on-Spalding Moor for the annual Memorial service beautifully taken by a young RAF Padre and as always very moving.

At 11.00 hrs. precisely a magnificent Fly-past Salute by a single RAF Tucano flown by F/Lt Nick Graham.

Mac read the first Lesson and Edward Braide, who had won the 76 Squadron school prize 7 years ago, read the second.

Wreathes of poppies were laid by the very young and by the very old. A Naval Attaché from the Norwegian embassy, Commander Lars Fjell, who had joined us late on the Saturday evening, laid a wreath of poppies to honour Norwegians who had died fighting with the Squadron, part of the 800 men of 76 Squadron who never came back.

We then moved to the little village school "adopted" by the old 76 Squadron Association where, to a background of coffee and biscuits, Lars presented a cheque from the old Squadron Association to the Headmaster – the annual Squadron donation to the school. This was followed by an excellent lunch at the Red Lion.

Finally, a long wet drive home – all thanks to James who drove through appalling weather and traffic with the eye and skill of a Tucano pilot. A wonderful weekend and I believe the right time to say "Goodbye" to five memorable years of my life at the age of 22.

Looking back on a long and happy life I see three outstanding reasons. The first and second stand unchallenged. My wife and my family.

One morning in 1950 I was sitting in the canteen of Airways Terminal, Victoria and thinking of little else but the coffee. Coming down the stairs in the blue uniform of BOAC (British Overseas Airways Corporation) the most beautiful girl I had ever seen. When in uniform she always wore a little red waistcoat with brass buttons. Unofficial of course but perfect.

Mary, Charles' wife

We were married on the last day of March the following year in 1951 in Owermoigne church Dorset by my Father, the Rector.

For 62 years I have known the truth of what I saw that day on the stairs so long ago. The unparalleled happiness that family life can give.

Finally, the third reason – the strength of friendships through the years.

For their dedicated work, patience in the handling of an old man, and unfailing good humour may I thank my daughters Rosanne and Kate for making this book possible.

To Mary and my daughter Caroline for their immediate help whenever asked and frequently needed.

Finally to my grandchildren Elizabeth, David, Marianna, Richard, Eleanor, Joe and Rosie and great grandchildren Talon and Pasha-Rose, for their very own and delightful contributions often unknown to them at the time.

This little book is written in the hope that it will give our children, grandchildren and great-grandchildren a glimpse of a different world in the days when we were young.

BATTLEFIELD TOUR FOR VETERANS

Goodwood – Caen – Pegasus Bridge, Friday 11th Sept 2015

David Hewings

David Hewings, Chairman of the Bognor Regis RAF Association Branch, to whom we owe so much for the arrangements of the trip, writes:

World War 2 Veterans Returned To France

Three RAF veterans found themselves on a flight back to France on the 11th September 2015, thanks to the generosity and courtesy of Conciair Flight Charter Ltd.

Charles and Mary

Flying low level over the D Day landing beaches, on a Battlefield Tour, the veterans landed at Caen.

They then travelled to the famous Pegasus Bridge for refreshments with Madame Gondrée, who as a young girl, witnessed the capture of the bridge from the Germans in 1944.

Tony, Barry, John, Joe, Mary and Charles

After further visits to other WW2 historical sites in the company of a professional tour guide, our intrepid veterans returned to Goodwood.

For Selsey resident Joe Roddis, who was an RAF engine fitter on Spitfires at RAF Westhampnett, it was a repeat of his flight just a few days after D-Day from the airfield to Caen in 1944, to prepare for his Squadron's arrival after the Luftwaffe was driven out. Joe has appeared in two documentaries on the Battle of Britain, one with David Jason and the other with John Sargeant and is the subject of the book by Mark Hillier entitled, "In Support of the Few".

Tony, Barry, Mde Gondrée, John, Joe, Mary and Charles

Another veteran and Branch 381 member, accompanied by his wife Mary, was Charles Gallagher DFC. He trained as a Navigator/Bomb Aimer in South Africa and then completed 29 Operations as a Bomb Aimer on the four engine Halifax Bomber. Returning from a raid in badly damaged aircraft, he and the crew opted to stay with their pilot, Walter "Mac" MacFarlane DFC, instead of bailing out. All survived the war and Charles and Mac went to India and Far East after 76 Squadron converted to Dakotas, ferrying supplies and assisting in the return of Allied POW's. They remain close friends to this day. Unfortunately Mac was not able to go on this flight and Mary took his place. Ill health prevented this exceptional duo taking to the skies together over Europe for one last time.

The Royal Navy was also represented by John Lewcock and Barry Bishop both of whom saw service in the treacherous Battle of the Atlantic. John joined the Navy in 1944 and served on HM Ships Albion, Victorious, Ark Royal and Hermes. As a raw recruit he was flown along the Normandy Beaches to be given a privileged view of the action just after D Day. He went on to play his part in the campaigns off Malaysia before WWII ended, Borneo and East Africa. Barry served from 1940 on HM Destroyers Chesterfield and Newark.

Also in the party was Life Vice President Tony Sheraton. He joined the RAF shortly after WWII ended. He initially served with 230 Squadron operating the Supermarine Sea Otter in support of the North Greenland Expedition. He took part in the parade for the Coronation of Queen Elizabeth in 1953. He is also responsible for the photographs that accompany this article.

The Battlefield Tour Guide was Col Mike Bradley OBE. His 40 years of service in the Army has been followed by 15 years as a guide across the world, from France and Germany to Burma and Malaysia.

Col Mike Bradley

During the trip, Charles laid a wreath at the Ranville War Cemetery.

Charles laying wreath

Barry, Charles, Joe, Mary, John and Tony

Being the first day of the Goodwood Revival, there was a lot of activity on the airfield when they returned. Immediately after their aircraft landed there was a mass take-off of 20 odd WWII fighters, mainly Spitfires and Hurricanes. From where they were on the airfield, they were able to watch the following air display so close, as Charles put it, "You could almost touch them". A fitting tribute to veterans who played such an important part in ensuring we have the freedom we have today.

Our veterans then returned home. Well that was all but 95 year old Joe Roddis, who was last seen disappearing across the airfield in a cloud of dust in a Willy's Jeep!

Charles, Mary, Barry, Joe, Mike (rear), John and Tony

D-DAY AND THE NORMANDY LANDINGS

After my visit to Pegasus Bridge I was talking with Elodie, my grandson David's partner.

Elodie

From our discussion I realized that her childhood years were spent in Normandy and I asked her to send me her thoughts and those of her relatives who lived through the years of occupation. Along with these she also sent her own beautiful painting of the battle area.

Elodie writes,

I have been living in the UK for more than 10 years, but I am from Normandy, in the north west of France. I was born in Caen, and grew up a few kilometers north of it, near the coast. Whenever somebody asks me where I am from, they will more often than not, upon my reply, start talking to me about D-Day. The fact that 73 years after it took place, this event still resonates so much in people's minds says a lot about how remarkable an achievement it was. Maybe because it is after all, pretty recent, or maybe because it has been immortalized in literature, films, TV shows, documentaries and therefore is now part of popular culture.

Charles has always been keen to ask me about D-Day and the Battle of Normandy, and I have always been happy to share what I have learnt about it throughout the years. You would find that most people in Normandy are pretty knowledgeable about it – it is unavoidable. As children, we learn about it in history class, we take school trips to museums and bunkers. There are war cemeteries and memorials and monuments pretty much everywhere. Our streets and squares and buildings are named after it. There are commemorations every year, with veterans and parades and head of states and reconstructions. And we all know someone who knows someone who did this or saw that on D-Day.

When I heard that he and his lovely Mary were taking a day trip to Normandy, I was delighted, because they were going to fly above and visit places I know very well, which Charles would find very interesting; but also because Normandy has a special place in its heart for WW2 veterans, and so providing the weather would be kind to them, they were going to have a wonderful time.

I am from Calvados, on the eastern side of Normandy, and grew up in Douvres – very near Gold, Juno and Sword, the sites of British and Canadian landings. My family though, is from the department of La Manche, on the western side of the region, and they were liberated by American soldiers advancing from the Utah and Omaha landing beaches.

My paternal grandmother – the only grandparent I have left – refuses to talk about the war. She was born in 1927, so she was 17 years old on D-Day. Whenever we bring it up, she changes the subject. Broadly speaking, there seem to be two attitudes from people who have lived throughout the Occupation and the Liberation when they are asked about it: they will either be silent like my grandmother, or the opposite – talk about it at great length, repeating the same stories in crystal clear details. For example, Monsieur Hervieu, a family friend, who was 12 years old in the summer of 1944, tearfully remembers the American soldier at his bedroom window who was shooting enemy soldiers hidden between the rows of peas and beans in his parent's garden – 'taking them out one by one'. He is haunted by this scene, and by the vision of German corpses lined up on the side of the road they took when American troops evacuated him and his family out of their village on that day. He has carried with him the memory of the sights and sounds and smells of war for more than seventy years – it makes me understand why my grandma would not want to think or talk about it, as frustrating as it might be for us not to know what her experiences were like.

One thing that we do know is that she, too, was evacuated to the coast line while the worst of the fighting took place. The same goes for Louis, the man who would later become my grandfather. He was also 17 years old at the time – too young to fight or be conscripted to mandatory work in Germany. His father, my great-grandpa, was a WW1 veteran who had fought in the trenches of Verdun in 1916. By the time the Second World War was declared, he was too old to fight and stayed on his farm with his family during the occupation. How bitter it must have been for him to see France fall to Germany after the sacrifices he had made in his younger years to prevent exactly that. They were evacuated in July 1944, and when they came back, they found that a hole had been made at the back of their house, and covered with sticks and twigs: their home had been used as a lookout to the surrounding fields by German soldiers. My grandma still lives in this house. Although it has of course been repaired, you can still see exactly where this hole was, and the bullet holes in the tiles and corrugated iron sheets that make up the roof of the old barn right next to it.

A couple of years later, my grandfather was sent to do his military service to Landau, in the French-occupied zone of Germany. He spent two years there, 'cleaning up Germany' as he called it. It is also where my dad was sent to do his military service 25 years later – France kept a base there until the late 1980s.

On my mother's side though, things were a bit different. My maternal grandparents were older at the outbreak of the war. My grandpa Henri was called up and served on the French front in Alsace (in the Maginot line area) for 8 months before being sent home after the birth of his third child, not long before France capitulated and the occupation began. His two younger brothers, along with many young men of the village, were conscripted to go and work in Germany, on a state-farm. Both my great uncles escaped, hid and somehow came back after the Liberation, telling tales of slavery, violence and starvation. A neighbour, Leon, who was there until the end of the war, remembered the torture of having to produce food while not being allowed to eat it. He once got delirious and ate soap, just to have something in his stomach. He recalled an incident where beets went missing, and as there was no culprit to be found, German soldiers threatened to summarily execute a father of two. A priest confessed to the theft, and was shot instead. Whether he was actually guilty or not is anyone's guess.

My grandparents were lucky enough to have a large garden and grow some food, and they just about managed to make do with what they had. There was also rationing. According to my grandmother Suzanne, the Wehrmacht soldiers were not too bad to deal with at the beginning of the occupation. They were fairly old – WW1 veterans, strict but fair. She recalled one in particular who had taken a liking to my baby aunt, and who had explained to them in broken French that he too had a baby daughter of her age back in his country. As time went by though, they were replaced by much younger, more zealous soldiers. By the end of it, German kids as young as 16-17 years old were occupying this corner of La Manche. They tended to help themselves in people's houses and gardens, and terrorized the locals.

I remember that all four of my grandparents had this habit, to conclude a nice meal, to put a hand on their stomach and spitefully declare 'another one the Germans won't get!'. My grandma still does it sometimes, because she knows it will make us smile. The expression, learnt from their parents and which became popular after WW1, always made us children laugh, as it sounds so absurd, and we were completely oblivious to the meaning it carries. When we thought about the dangers of the war, we thought about fighting and bullets and evil nazis. It never occurred to us that hunger was a common, everyday enemy, which they had to endure for years. It is a strange thing for people of my generation to think about a good meal as revenge; a full stomach, a victory.

In my parents' house, on an elaborate wrought iron and wooden stand, sits an antique Howe sewing machine. It is more than a century old, and has not been used in decades, yet it still is in perfect working order. As a child I loved to sit between the legs of the stand and turn the wheel which activated the heavy pedal. I was not allowed to lift the lid – it's a perfect trap for little fingers – but I could see the mechanical parts moving together from below, and found it fascinating.

This sewing machine belonged to my great-grandmother Julia, who was a seamstress. It was her working tool, and that alone would be enough to give it great sentimental value, but what makes it even more precious is the fact that it is the one material possession Julia had left after her city, Coutances, was liberated from German occupation in July 1944.

The allied forces had landed in Lower Normandy a month before that. The American progression had been slow – this part of Normandy was (and still is) very rural, with a variety of wooded countryside, fields, and marshlands which provided defensive positions favorable for ambushes by an enemy much more familiar with the terrain. This first month of American advance in La Manche is referred to as 'La Bataille des Haies' – the 'War of the Hedges' because of the numerous hedges, ditches and bushes adorning the Norman bocage. The territory had to be conquered one field at a time, which was not only very time-consuming but also very costly in lives. I was taught at school that in some sectors, statistically, for every meter of advance, the American army lost one man – 1000 per kilometre. Incredible.

And so, getting back to Julia – more than a month after D-Day, Coutances was still a German occupied city. At the end of July started Operation Cobra, aiming at breaking through German defenses and advancing towards Brittany, effectively driving the German army towards the east and the British and Canadian forces.

The American carpet bombing of the Coutances region began, and two thirds of the city was destroyed. My great-grandmother stayed there until her house started to burn. She left in a hurry, and walked the ten kilometres that separated her from my grandparents' house with nothing but the clothes on her back. Once she was safe and settled there, my grandfather got on his bike and rode to Coutances, to find out that her home was now a pile of rubble and ashes, and the only thing that made it in one piece was the solid metal sewing machine, which he tied to the back of his bike and took back to Julia. I can only imagine what it must have been like for him, to have to tell her that pretty much everything she had was gone.

When the American bombing intensified, my grandparents and their family went to find refuge in a nearby barn. A bomb fell down into a pit of manure right next to it. My uncle André, who would have been twelve or thirteen years old at the time, was nowhere to be found for a few hours after that. My grandmother thought that they had lost him and convinced herself that he was either dead or dying at the bottom of a well next to the landing site of the bomb. He was found eventually, remarkably uninjured but in shock, having been projected many metres away by the blast into bushes of stinging nettles. Funnily enough, nettle stings are the one thing he still recalls vividly about that day. My aunt, who was a baby at the time, was wounded by shrapnel on her forehead in the same explosion. She received treatment for that injury by the GI's who swept the area a few hours later, and evacuated the civilians who had remained.

My maternal grandparents had a neighbour, Emma, who received an award for her bravery during the war. An American plane had crashed in one of the nearby fields and she had found the parachuted pilot injured, but alive, not far from it. When German soldiers showed up to investigate, she somehow managed to pass the bandaged man as her son. How she got away with that, I do not know – but she did, and when he was well enough, she entrusted him with the local postmaster, a member of the resistance, who helped him rejoin the closest American outpost.

My grandmother was bitter about Emma, and her medal. Thinking about it, I understand why now – Emma got lucky. Had she got caught – to be honest, I am not sure how she did not – she would have been executed on the spot, her family too, and any neighbour who may or may not have been involved as well.

After many aerial raids and bombings at the beginning of the year, a large amount of German reinforcements had arrived in Normandy in March 1944. Reprisals were common and the D-Day landings only made the situation more volatile, the occupying troops more zealous.

Emma had risked many lives to save one, and my grandmother never forgave her for that. To make things worse, the soldier in question was back on a plane a few weeks later, and got shot down again. This time he did not make it – he is buried in the Saint James cemetery in Normandy. There was of course no way of knowing things would turn out the way they did – but my grandmother had an 'all of this for that' attitude about it which sounds pretty harsh out of context. This is something that I could not understand as a child – but I do now. There were more than enough dangers to think about for my grandparents and their young family, without their neighbour bringing more to their doorstep.

The fact is, we all would like to think that we would be brave in such situations. But we cannot know that for sure. History and culture have a tendency to focus on extremes – heroes and villains. My grandparents were neither – like millions of other civilians throughout Europe during this conflict, they were ordinary people who had to live through extraordinary circumstances. Of course, they are heroes to me – bravery comes in many forms, and when Charles asked me to write about this and I started asking my family about these stories, I found myself admiring my grandparents for their resilience, often thinking to myself that I would never have been able to recover from all of this the way that they did. By the time I was born, they were loving, fun, sweets-giving, jam-making grandparents, rich with an appreciation of life that can only be acquired through living and surviving the traumatic events they had to endure. It is a particular kind of wisdom that I also find in Charles and Mary.

As difficult as it has been for me to look into this, and write about it, I feel that I got to know my grandparents better, and I am indeed very proud of them all.

76 SQUADRON - CENTENARY YEAR

The Squadron was formed in the Home Defence Force of the Royal Flying Corps on the 15th of September 1916.

The Reserve Squadron Association most kindly invited us to the celebration weekend at Linton-on-Ouse on the weekend of the 16th September 2016.

James, Mac's son, once again drove Mary and me up to Linton, picking up Mac on the way.

Mac and James

We left early morning, arriving at the Linton Guardroom early evening, to be met by the other part of the family who were able to come.

Caroline, my eldest daughter, had travelled by train from West Sussex, joined by her son Richard, and Rosie, my granddaughter, who had jumped on the train in London to travel on to Linton together!

Supper in the Officer's Mess, followed by an early night for several rather tired travellers.

On the Saturday morning we woke to a perfect English day, bound for Middleton St George – an early base of the Squadron during the war. We gathered in the Memorial room on getting there. Then followed a most interesting sight of the room and its contents.

And finally an excellent lunch – very heartily enjoyed by all!

After lunch, back to the cars and to Linton-on-Ouse to their Memorial room and a most interesting talk and discussion on it's fascinating contents.

A great day, and on arrival back at the Officer's Mess at Linton we were greeted by my youngest daughter, Kate, who had just arrived to join us. We plunged immediately into a superb dinner party organized brilliantly by Martin Wintermeyer to whom we owe a wonderful weekend.

Sunday dawned and after a good night's sleep we drove from Linton to the little church standing on the hill overlooking both the village and airfield of Holme-on-Spalding-Moor. We headed for the Service of Remembrance arriving spot on 11 o'clock – to a very warm welcome from the congregation.

Richard, my grandson, unbeknown to me at the time, was asked to read the first Lesson as the person assigned to do it had been held up by traffic and was late. He did it beautifully – it was a very proud moment.

Richard

At the end of a beautiful Service the entire congregation moved to the Squadron window, hugely approved by all.

Charles and Mac

As we left the church we were met by the full glory of a perfect English autumn day – Yorkshire just showing off.

Mac and I sat for a few moments together, enjoying this wonderful day, remembering the old days of the Crew.

As we walked down the hill to our cars, a final glance at the church which had maintained a watch for the returning Crews throughout the long years of the war – and I believe perhaps continues an eternal vigil for the 780 men who had never come back.

We visited the little village school at Holme-on-Spalding-Moor whose children had created an exhibition of poetry, art and craft work in honour of the Squadron and its connection with the school. This was most beautifully done and hugely valued by us.

Charles admiring art work

111

Mac and I had a great chat with the school's head teacher, Helen Ross, enabling my Book "Memories of a Different World" to make a donation to the school.

I have always been personally delighted with the association between the Squadron and the school.

Following our great visit to the school we went to the memorial on our old Airfield.

May my final thoughts be concerned entirely with the overwhelming importance of the Centenary Service of Remembrance that took place there where a small boy shook my hand; he must have been around 8 years old, the same age as my great grandson Talon.

Mac and I had the privilege of standing together, being able to share with a part of both our families in our final salute to the Squadron, the Command and the Royal Air Force.

Some of the great moments of my life.

ALL SAINTS CHURCH
HOLME-UPON-SPALDING MOOR
76 SQUADRON MEMORIAL WINDOW

76 Squadron R A F - Memorial Window
All Saints, Holme - On - Spalding Moor, York

The Squadron badge is shown prominently in the right-hand light of the window and below it are shown three anchors, a reminder of the losses suffered during action against the German capital ships:- Scharnhorst, Gneisenau and Tirpitz.

All Saints Church itself is depicted in the left-hand light, with the red beacon shining from the tower against a lightening night sky, in which are shown a handful of stars.

The main central area of the design is composed of two large interlinked circles. The upper edge of the top circle represents the sun rising, (dawn breaking) and the lower edge of the lower circle is marked as for a compass rose. The central area represents the landscape of Yorkshire, in which the Church sits, and the airfield of Holme-upon-Spalding Moor, and for which (as part of our country) our armed forces fought and in some cases lost their lives.

At the top of the right-hand light are shown two Halifax bombers returning from Ops, guided in over the early morning fields towards the airfield by the red beacon.

The Hercules radial engine is shown at the base of the right-hand light, and balancing on the left, the up-turned faces of two ground crew, awaiting the returning aircraft. The words "TO SEE THE DAWN BREAKING – SAFELY HOLME" (this is the title of the Squadron's History) are shown between the Church and their faces.

The yellow lines in the lower half of each light depict the runways of the airfield. An extract from a poem written by Minnie Louise Haskins (b. 1874 – d. 1957) is written on the lower part of the right-hand light and the words "In memory of 76 Squadron R.A.F." are at the base of the left-hand light.

The text of the poem is an extract from "GOD KNOWS" and is as follows:-

And I said to the man who stood at the gate of the year:
'Give me a light that I may tread safely into the unknown'
And he replied:
'Go out into the darkness and put your hand into the hand
of God.
That shall be to you better than light and safer than a
known way.'

This window was dedicated on September 4th 1994. The design is by Ann Sotheran of York.

HIGH FLIGHT

Oh! I have slipped the surly bonds of Earth
And danced the skies on laughter-silvered wings;
Sunward I've climbed, and joined the tumbling mirth
Of sun-split clouds, – and done a hundred things

You have not dreamed of – wheeled and soared and swung
High in the sunlit silence. Hov'ring there,
I've chased the shouting wind along, and flung
My eager craft through footless halls of air....

Up, up the long, delirious, burning blue
I've topped the wind-swept heights with easy grace.
Where never lark, or even eagle flew –
And, while with silent lifting mind I've trod,

The high untrespassed sanctity of space
-Put out my hand and touched the face of GOD.

by Pilot Officer John G. Magee Jr.
An American citizen who gave his life
with the Royal Canadian Air Force